THE
POWER
OF
ST. JOSEPH

FIVE REASONS WHY HE IS
TERROR OF DEMONS
(AND HOW YOU CAN BE ONE TOO)

THE
POWER
OF
ST. JOSEPH

FIVE REASONS WHY HE IS
TERROR OF DEMONS
(AND HOW YOU CAN BE ONE TOO)

DEVIN SCHADT

ISBN: 978-1-7358464-1-5
Stewardship: A Mission of Faith
11 BlackHawk Lane
Elizabethtown, PA 17022
StewardshipMission.org

To Joe:

A most patient teacher,

a superior Thomist,

a scourge of heretics,

and a most faithful friend.

TABLE OF CONTENTS

St. Joseph,
Terror of Demons

I'm a big fan and disciple of St. Joseph. Approximately two decades ago, I began entrusting myself to his care and guidance. I discovered him to be more than an intercessor, but rather a mentor and spiritual father. The spiritual riches that he bestows on those who entrust themselves to his fatherly protection are abundant and never wanting.

Initially, what I knew about St. Joseph was not all that impressive. By all appearances he seemed to be somewhat weak, apprehensive, a placeholder, if you will, who filled the slot of being a substitute father, making the awkward situation of the Virgin Mary's teenage pregnancy appear acceptable.

The homilies I had heard regarding St. Joseph described him as a man who, like many men of our time, wanted to divorce his wife and be relieved of a difficult situation.

The challenge to understanding St. Joseph was primarily due to the silence and obscurity that surrounded him. There was so little information about him. To really know him seemed nearly impossible.

On the other hand, I encountered devotionals, booklets, and other literature in which the authors attempted to make up for the lack of available information about St. Joseph by rendering him like God Himself, describing him in such lofty esteem that he seemed untouchable and unrelatable.

In these resources I discovered a common thread. Typically, the author would identify a virtue or an attribute worthy of admiration and graft it onto the person of St. Joseph, without using the divinely inspired Sacred Scripture as the basis of their view. The authors would appeal to what people said about St. Joseph, but neglect to reflect on what Scripture actually said about him.

This is a common, recurring theme that began with the apocryphal accounts of St. Joseph.[1] It is from these traditions that legendary ideas of St. Joseph snowballed and became more widely accepted and retold.

After all, anything said about him seemed too little, given that he was the husband of the Blessed Virgin Mary and the foster father of Jesus, the Son of God. It made the sky the limit in describing how St. Joseph perfectly embodies every virtue.

For example, if the Litany of St. Joseph says that he is Mirror of Patience, an author will pay him the greatest tribute regarding his patience and long-suffering. They describe the virtue of patience in great detail, without referencing in particular how Scripture recounts him embodying this saintly characteristic.

There is a difference between exegesis and eisegesis. Exegesis means to draw out the meaning that Scripture itself is proposing, while eisegesis is arriving at our own conclusions, based on our own preferences and considerations, then applying them to or grafting them onto the scriptural passage. The former is like a rose opening to give you a view of what is inside, whereas the latter is like spray-painting gold glitter on the closed rose's petals.

There are countless books about St. Joseph that are saturated with eisegesis. This doesn't necessarily mean that the thoughts and ideas contained in these sources are untrue.

Often, they are true, but they lack the expressed biblical basis for the truth. The ideas are not born from Scripture but added onto them superficially.

Last summer, I was asked to give a talk at a Catholic family conference on St. Joseph, outlining why he is Terror of Demons. I immediately agreed, because I had so much material to support the idea of St. Joseph as Terror of Demons. "This will be easy," I thought.

Preparing for the talk, I jotted down approximately twenty-five compelling reasons why St. Joseph was Terror of Demons. As powerful and descriptive as these reasons were, I was convinced that I too was grafting or inserting my own ideas about St. Joseph on him, instead of St. Joseph opening my mind to who he actually is, based on divine revelation.

Suddenly, I began to sweat. What does Scripture really say about St. Joseph? Further, does any of what is mentioned give us compelling and convincing reasons to support the idea of Joseph being able to terrorize demons? No longer was I excited about giving the blessed talk.

Sure, I could have said that because St. Joseph was head of the Holy Family, that was reason enough to scare the demons back to Hell where they belong. Though this is true, it didn't help me convey the real St. Joseph and it didn't propose an example that we could imitate.

As I so often do, in desperation I crawled on bended knee to God, begging the Holy Spirit to impart to me the wisdom and truth regarding the real St. Joseph; and, if there existed reasons why he is Terror of Demons, that He would disclose them to me.

The heavenly floodgates opened, and that's why this book now exists.

Though the biblical passages concerning St. Joseph are few, the Holy Spirit led me to discover within these scriptures the important truths that God intends to say about St. Joseph. Though I am no scholar, academic, or theologian, God revealed to me pieces of the mystery of St. Joseph that lay hidden in the Hebrew, Greek, and Latin words that described him.

There is a wealth of inspired revelation regarding St. Joseph, but I chose to focus on those attributes that are fundamental to the human person—five characteristics of St. Joseph that each human being can imitate and embody in their pursuit of conquering evil and becoming a living saint.

I turned to St. Thomas Aquinas in hopes that he might have something to say regarding these attributes. Did he ever. Though St. Thomas was not referring to St. Joseph directly, the five attributes contained in his Summa Theologica were a large part of the fundamental attributes of the virtuous man.

I realize this might sound somewhat abstract and inaccessible. Though Sacred Scripture and St. Thomas's incredible insights are the basis of our thoughts regarding St. Joseph, this book displays these five attributes in a very approachable and practical way that you can put to work in your own life.

Why is this important? Because the devil, unfortunately, has tremendous influence over many of us—even so-called good Catholics—and most of us don't even realize it.

Often, we lack the power and ability to penetrate people's hearts with Christ's saving proclamation of the Gospel because we barely embody that saving grace ourselves.

We love Jesus, but estimate that the Gospel is limited in its power to give us peace, joy, happiness, and freedom; and consequently we appeal to the world's power to obtain these things. Yet, without realizing it, though we think we are mastering this power, this power is mastering us.

We envision ourselves as bold for Christ, but when we are faced with the world's version of virtue, such as "getting along," "equality," "niceness," "inclusiveness," "toleration," "freedom," and "diversity," we jump aboard the world's *Titanic* and sail along with the sea's southbound current.

In this little book you will discover that St. Joseph is **not** a benign nice guy who loves lily flower arrangements. Nor will you get a glittery, shiny image of St. Joseph. You will discover how St. Joseph's five core attributes relate to your life, your happiness, and how you interpret and respond to current social issues like transgenderism; social media bullying and boasting; the pursuit of glory; equality; homosexual unions; separation of Church and state; anger and the passions; contraception; the government's restrictions on religious gatherings and the shutting down of Catholic churches.

St. Joseph's five core virtues flip our common, comfortable, world view on its illogical head, and give us the practical wisdom needed to obtain and embody the power of God Almighty.

This book is not a campaign to laud the glories of St. Joseph. It is a deeper look at the real St. Joseph; a heroic, faithful man who fought tooth and nail for his wife, his family, and his God. It is a practical guide to help you unlock the power necessary to become like St. Joseph, Terror of Demons.

CHAPTER 1

Real Power

Power. We all want it. We all could use more of it. And almost always, we sense that we never have enough of it. Yet most of us would never admit, at least aloud, that we desire to have more power and want to be powerful.

Imagine yourself having a warm, casual conversation with a longtime friend. Somewhere during the conversation you thoughtfully interject, "You know, Betty, I want to be powerful . . . I mean really powerful." Betty, now looking like she was stunned by a taser, peers back at you with a blinkless gaze of horror. She eyes the door as she thinks, "My kind, lifelong friend is actually Napoleon, a monster chomping at the bit, waiting for his moment to conquer the world."

The truth is that, though Betty may not be able to articulate it, she has a similar desire. She wants power . . . and a lot of it. We all do.

Public speakers want the effect of emotionally influencing their audiences. The financial investor desires to have mastery over his finances and portfolio, and yours. Personal life-coaches want to motivate you to be your greatest, thus making them greater. Parents want better control over their children and their behavior. Computer engineers, graphic designers, and videographers want to be more proficient with their software applications. The parish priest longs for his parishioners to follow his lead. The mid-forties man with the "dad bod" wants control over his weight. Small business owners want their employees to carry out their vision promptly and with excellence. The boyfriend flatters his girlfriend in order to acquire her affection. Politicians desire to control the vote and also the citizen. Social media platforms give you the power to reach the masses, and after you have come to depend on that reach, those platforms and apps have power over you.

Whether you are a parent, a professional athlete, a rodeo rider, a city plow truck driver, a meteorologist, a CEO, a COO, a politician, a engineer, or aspoiled kid, we all want power sometimes over ourselves, almost always over others, and always over things, conditions, outcomes, and the course of events.

That is precisely what power is. Power is defined as the ability to direct or influence the behavior of others or the course of events. Power is the ability to produce an effect. Power is the possession of control, authority, and influence over others. Power is physical might, mental or moral efficacy. Power is the ability to motivate, manipulate, and control. Who couldn't use a little more of that?

Power, however, is a dangerous thing, difficult to wield; in some cases it can betray us, causing us and others untold harm.

Perhaps J.R.R. Tolkien, in his epic trilogy, *The Lord of the Rings*, has most persuasively portrayed and iconized power with the "Ring of Power." Sauron, the great dark lord, squeezed all of his malicious power into the "One Ring to Rule Them All." Every creature that gains possession of it is eventually taken possession by it. Whether it is Ilsidur, the former King of Gondor, Gollum, or even Frodo, the power that the ring gave them, also gave the ring power over them.

21

At one point, in the first book of the trilogy, *The Fellowship of the Ring*, Lord Elrond holds a private council, which includes elves, dwarves, hobbits, a wizard, and men, to decide the fate of the One Ring.

Frodo, the current ringbearer, who successfully brought the One Ring to Elrond and Rivendell, during the council, in sight of those attending, places the Ring of Power on a stone table. A sudden excitement and desire is awakened in the attending members. Boromir, the son of the Steward of the kingdom of Gondor, who has battled against Sauron's forces, rises from his chair, stands amidst the council members, and says, "It [the One Ring] is a gift. A gift to the foes of Mordor (the kingdom of Sauron) . . . Why not use this ring?" Later, when Boromir is tempted to take the ring from Frodo, he mutters, "It is a strange fate that we should suffer so much fear and doubt over so small a thing, such a little thing."

From this point on Boromir is consumed with obtaining the Ring of Power for himself, and it is this desire that eventually leads to his ruin. Boromir believes that an evil means (the ring) could be wielded to produce a good and righteous end. He was convinced that *he* could manage and manipulate its power without being manipulated. And why not? After all, it is such a little thing.

Here lies the tremendous, deceptive character of worldly power. It often presents itself in the little package of a white lie, an imperceptible theft, a hidden immoral act that "will never hurt anyone."

Don't be fooled.

Attempt to use it and it could use you, try to possess it and eventually it will possess you. How can that be? If God's power is unerring and we use His good power, we, and the power ought to be good—like God. Yet, power itself without God's goodness becomes disordered or, at worst, evil. This is what worldly power is: power that lacks God's goodness. In other words, when imperfect humans misuse a perfect power, they render that power imperfect. It's like using a magnifying lens not to help yourself see better, but to channel sunlight directly onto an ant, torturing and burning it. You can see the agony of the ant better, but you used the magnifying glass primarily to torture the ant.

Aristotle said that pleasure can be good but can become bad when we seek pleasure for its own sake. An example of this would be pursuing the pleasure of taste and obtaining food for that purpose alone. The pleasurable taste associated with food is a good thing, but if my sole purpose is to experience taste while disconnecting it from the other noble purposes of food, such as nutrition, affording social harmony (a good time with others around a meal), a consolation to overcome tension, or gratification after achieving a goal, such as a hard day's work, I am committing or will eventually commit the sin of gluttony (not to mention compromising my pancreas' ability to process sugar).

Another example of how pursuing pleasure for its sake alone becomes disordered and damages people is sexual intercourse. God created sexual intercourse to be incredibly pleasurable. The pleasure, though, is not the purpose of sexual intercourse but a consequence of it. The divine purpose of sexual intercourse is unity between the couple and fruitfulness of a child. But if a couple has casual sex (sexual intercourse without any kind of commitment), or sexual intercourse outside of the marital bond, or without being open to conceiving a child, the good purpose of sexual intercourse is rejected in pursuit of the consequence of pleasure alone. When people have intercourse for the sake of pleasure itself, one or both of the persons involved become objectified, used, and wounded.

Power is similar to pleasure. Power, like pleasure, is morally neutral, but can be used for good or evil. If we seek power for its own sake, that power will become disordered, sinful, and evil. This is what Christians call worldly power, a power that is under the ruler of this world, the devil. In our efforts to channel worldly power we run the risk of being channeled by it.

Nevertheless, we often attempt to obtain power for its own sake, or to use power for a selfish goal, believing that it is the most effective means to procure a good outcome.

The tax-evader illegally shelters his money from the government to ensure that his child is provided for financially. The parish priest neglects to preach about the controversial truths of Christ for the purpose of keeping the collections rolling in. The young lady dresses scantily to attract a hoped-for future husband. The social media detractor reveals the sins of others in order to protect the public good. The business owner cooks the books to ensure that the sale of his enterprise goes through. A couple shacks up prior to being married to "test-drive" the relationship and make sure it works.

The husband uses contraception to ensure that his wife, who is the mother of his six children, won't become pregnant and lose her wits. The love-starved female flirts with her married co-worker to obtain male affirmation. The college student aborts her child so she can obtain her degree and not sabotage her potential future career. A husband imagines other, more attractive, naked women in order to become aroused by his wife. You get the idea.

All of these people have two things in common: first, they misuse power by sacrificing a higher good for a lesser good; or by sacrificing a wholistic good for a partial good (we will explain this more soon). Second, they believe that by using power in this way, they can obtain happiness.

We all want happiness (the ultimate good). We cannot help but want it because we are made for it. God, who is happiness itself, created us to be with Him for all eternity, which means that He made us to be happy. Happiness is every human being's "North Star." We are magnetically drawn to its brilliant light.

This is precisely why we all, at one time or another, fall for the temptation to do something we know is immoral, or to use a questionable means to procure love, intimacy, stability, success, prestige, honor, popularity, pleasure, and the like. We do this because we equate these things with happiness.

Quite often happiness appears to be just out of reach. For example, an acquaintance's daughter has struggled for years to find Mr. Right. In a moment of desperation, she reduces herself to posting provocative selfies on a hookup app, eventually causing her shame. Until then, she had played by the rules and did everything "by the book," yet fell short of obtaining that desired object, which she believed assured her of the happiness that she longed for. We've all been there.

Despite how much we may desire happiness, a good end does not justify using an evil means to attain it (see CCC 1753). The good end of happiness does not justify sinning to obtain it. Sinning cannot ultimately make us happy. My ex-neighbor wanted male affirmation and attention. So she turned her apartment into a brothel. She overdosed on drugs and ended up in the ER. What appeared to be momentary happiness induced by sin became the cause of incredible despair. Why does sinning thwart our goal of obtaining happiness? Because sin causes death (see

Rom 6:23), misery, self-hatred, loneliness, and eternal damnation. None of that sounds very happy.

So how can we use power in a way that is not sinful—in a way that will bring us true happiness?

Unfortunately, there is no bulletproof, fail-safe method to discern whether we are using something that is morally neutral in itself for evil or for good. There is only one occasion in which we can know that power is always rendered as evil, thus making an act sinful: when we use an intrinsic evil means to achieve an end goal. For example: I want to be wealthy. My neighbor is filthy rich and keeps an incredibly large amount of his money in his house safe. I hold him up at gunpoint, coerce him to unlock the safe, take his money, and murder him.

The goal—to become wealthy in an unjust way—is evil because the means and the objective (holding my neighbor up at gunpoint, murdering him, and stealing his money) are intrinsically evil. Such a case is very easy for the average human being to discern as evil, and yet such cases are infrequent and exceptional (though media outlets would have you believe otherwise).

To determine whether we are using power correctly in our common daily decisions demands effort and discernment.

And here lies the real problem. *Most people want to be happy, but most people don't want to work for it.* Most people don't want to put forth the effort to examine their actions and the motivations behind those actions. That is precisely why multitudes of humans miss the mark of happiness consistently. This is why so many of us repeatedly make poor decisions and end up consistently miserable.

The reason it is so difficult for us to discern whether we are using power correctly is because the majority of our actions involve using a means that is morally neutral—neither good nor bad—to attain our goal.

For example, a hammer is morally neutral. I can use a hammer to build a wheelchair ramp for a less fortunate person, or I can use that same hammer to bash in the skull of that person. In both cases, the hammer moves from being morally neutral to either a good means or an evil means of power.

A car can be used to deliver groceries to shut-ins or as a getaway car in a bank robbery. The car is no longer morally neutral in either case. In the former case it becomes a good means, and in the latter, it become an evil use of power.

Though there is no absolute rule, there are nevertheless consistent factors that can help us and our conscience use power correctly.

First, *the intention and the circumstances* will almost always determine whether we are using power correctly. If the intention of driving my car is to get to work, and I drive safely, obeying traffic laws, the intention and the circumstances are good. If my intention is to drive to work, but I am operating my vehicle while intoxicated, the intention may be good, but the means and the circumstances—being drunk while using a motor vehicle—is bad.

Sleep is normally good. If my intention is to sleep for the purpose of regenerating my brain in order to function well at my job, then sleep is good. If my intention is to oversleep for the purpose of avoiding facing my responsibilities, then sleep has become a means to committing the sin of sloth. So, intentions and circumstances are huge factors in determining whether we are using power correctly.

Second, we need to determine whether *the means that we use to obtain a good end are actually good.* Now there are two basic ways to determine if the means employed is good or evil. First, we are to never sacrifice a higher good for a lesser good.

For example, to sacrifice your marriage for the pleasure of a one-night stand would be to sacrifice a higher good for a lesser perceived good. Marriage is a sacrament that communicates God's grace, improving society; whereas infidelity transmits sin and destroys families, thus destroying society. Killing an unborn baby for the purpose of selling its body parts and stem cells to scientists who develop vaccines is sacrificing the higher good of human life, for the lesser good of *potentially* protecting human lives. An individual's human life is the higher good; potential human health is a lesser good.

Second, we never have the right to sacrifice a wholistic good for a partial good. For example, under persecution, a person may deny his belief in Jesus Christ to retain his possessions and freedom; but by doing so, he neglects the whole good of God and the purpose of his life: to live for God and for heaven. He retains the partial good of his possessions but loses the greater good of his salvation, and perhaps, by his bad example, leads others to imitate him.

Another example of this is committing genocide for the purpose of ensuring that generations to come will have enough resources. To kill people who are living today for the purpose of ensuring stability for the generations of tomorrow is trading a wholistic good of human life for a partial good of (potentially) providing for that human life. In other words, "An evil action cannot be justified by reference to a good intention" (Thomas Aquinas, Dec. praec. 6).

Besides examining our intention and the means and circumstances, a third way to determine whether our action is good or bad is to *assess whether the goal in itself is morally disordered.*

Beginning with a bad goal will inevitably involve an evil means and a misuse of power. For example, robbing a bank is a bad goal. The means to do it: a gun and a getaway car, were at one point morally neutral until they were used to threaten the bank teller and flee from the crime.

Becoming famous, or being honored, for its own sake is a bad goal, even if I use the means of donating large sums of money to the less fortunate to accomplish this goal. The means is actually good, but becomes disordered because of an evil goal: self-exaltation.

In other words, "A morally good act requires the goodness of its object, of its end, and its circumstances together" (CCC

1760). This is the closest we can get to a formula that helps us discern whether we are using power correctly.

"A good intention (for example, that of helping one's neighbor) does not make behavior that is intrinsically disordered, such as lying, or calumny, good or just . . . On the other hand, an added intention (such as vainglory) makes an act evil that in and of itself can be good (such as almsgiving)" (CCC 1753).

This should cause us to pause. In the world of instant communications, in the contexts of Facebook, Twitter, You-Tube, TikTok, and the like, how many of us are posting with the disordered motivation of vainglory, making our self-promotion unfit for God?

It is little wonder why so many of us feel dejected, demoralized, and humiliated by the lackluster amounts of hits, likes, view, comments, and followers we acquire. This sadness demonstrates that our motive is disordered, and that our intention is not to please God (the higher, wholistic good), but to please men (see Col 3:23).

So where do we go from here? Do we bury our heads in the sand and continue to misuse power and remain on the roller coaster that one moment allows us to flirt with the "high" of fleeting joy, and the next moment plummets us into utter misery and self-loathing? Or do we ignorantly believe that a Christian is not to be powerful, have power, or use power?

Not quite.

We need power, but not the power that the world, the flesh, and the devil offer. We need a power that is out of this world—we need God's power.

The Latin word for the power that God gives us for the purpose of achieving a good end goal is *virtus*. "Virtue in the Latin, *virtus*, signifies manliness or courage and can be understood as excellence of perfection due to a thing, just as vice, its contrary, denotes a defect or absence of perfection due to a thing."[2]

The etymology of the word *virtus* has its roots in the word "courage." But a more accurate definition of virtue is an *excellence of perfection*. In other words, any virtue, whether it be prudence, justice, temperance, modesty, purity, humility, mercy, or the like are cemented together and propelled by courage. Courage helps us to be virtuous. A person must be courageous to be just and be just to be courageous. Virtue cannot be maintained without courage, and courage without virtue is pride.

Virtue, then, is true power. Or, as my friend Joe says, "Virtue is power well-used."

So, the key to becoming saints, the key to conquering sin, the key to overcoming the temptation to use worldly power is for us not to seek power itself, but rather to seek virtue. *By obtaining virtue, you and I will have obtained true power.* If we seek power itself, we will eventually lack virtue, because we will be depending on worldly power rather than on God's power.

As one philosopher puts it, "Virtue is to bear suffering without becoming corrupt" (Jordan Peterson). In other words, while not every virtue is courage per se, every virtue demands courage to face suffering. *Virtue keeps a person from becoming corrupted by the misuse of worldly power.*

This is where power and virtue become very practical. Everyone suffers and will suffer. Yet everyone wants to be happy. The two states appear to be diametrically opposed. When you suffer you usually aren't happy, and if you are happy you usually aren't suffering. When the obstacle of suffering appears to block the path to happiness, we are gravely tempted to find a power, even a disordered, evil power, to remove that suffering, believing that it will bring us happiness. However, if we do use an evil power to remove suffering, we become corrupt and thus experience the worst type of suffering: self-hatred.

This is why we need real virtue: to carry out a good motivation to its good end. But to act virtuously demands courage. Virtue fortified by courage is necessary to achieve a noble and good goal in the face of temptation, adversity, depression, manipulation, and coercion.

This is the real power that will lead us to happiness and help us bring happiness to others. Again, virtuous acts demand great courage. Think: Jesus' agony in the garden, or Maximilian Kolbe ransoming a father by being executed in his place. Jesus and Maximilian Kolbe are truly powerful, because the world, the flesh, and the devil have no power over them. They faced tremendous evil with courage, acting virtuously, and because of this no one had power over their inner will. "For whatsoever is born of God, overcometh the world: and this is the victory which overcometh the world: our faith" (1 John 5:4).

Which brings us to an important point: if we are to overcome the temptation to use an immoral, disordered power to avoid pain and suffering, it is imperative that we have faith in God, believing that He will strengthen us with the courage to be victorious over evil. The man of faith has real power over sin, over Satan—and is a terror of demons.

What is a terror of demons? A terror of demons is a person whose motivations, goals, and the means they use to obtain those goals are godly and for God alone. The demons are terrorized by such men and women.

Counter that with a person who uses an illicit means to obtain a good end or uses a good end to hide a perverse motivation. The demons have no fear of such a person because he or she has become an ally or, worse, a slave to the demonic realm.

Returning once again to Tolkien's Ring of Power: if one attempted to use Sauron's One Ring for his own purpose, Sauron had power over that individual. Sauron had no need to fear Gollum or any ringbearer who exploited the Ring of Power.

Enter St. Joseph. One of the most powerful and provocative titles cited in the Litany of St. Joseph is Terror of Demons. St. Joseph was and is Terror of Demons par excellence because his motivations, goals, and the means to obtain those goals were good and holy. St. Joseph had godly goals, which he achieved for God alone.

St. Joseph exercised tremendous virtue and "bore suffering

without becoming corrupt." In the face of tremendous suffering, he avoided caving in to the temptation to use an immoral means to obtain a hoped-for solution. Because of this, St. Joseph was and is a real threat to the devil and his kingdom. St. Joseph is Terror of Demons.

Though Scripture appears to reveal very little about St. Joseph and his life, if we penetrate the surface of the Gospel and mine the sacred text, we discover a gold mine of illustrations of why he is Terror of Demons. For the sake of brevity, however, we will limit this little book to discussing five powerful ways that Joseph overcame the temptation to use worldly power to achieve a godly end.

Though St. Joseph's heroic example far surpasses most of our efforts, his five ways are very practical and applicable to each and every one of us in our daily lives.

Do you want real power in your life? Do you want to attain real happiness, the ultimate good? Would you like to be a terror of demons? The five ways that St. Joseph is Terror of Demons will provide you an exemplary "means" to obtain that good.

But be prepared for a mind shift. The power of St. Joseph

does not have the character of the loud and proud worldly power. The power of St. Joseph lacks selfish motives. In fact, at times his "power" will appear to be very weak.

St. Paul tells us "Though [Jesus] was crucified through weakness, yet He lives through the *power of God*. Yes, we are also weak in Him, yet we shall live with Him through the *power of God . . .*" (2 Cor 13:4). The Greek word for power used in this passage is "virtue." In other words, the power of God is virtue . . . and that's the kind of power we need.

Did you catch that? To be weak in Christ allows Christ to be powerful in us. St. Joseph will demonstrate that although your life's circumstances may make you feel weak—at times, even powerless—if you exercise virtue, which is God's power, His power will be manifest in and through you. And that's real power. After all, isn't that what we all want?

CHAPTER 2

Just Power

It was a Sunday morning, my youngest daughter's tenth birthday to be exact, when I was informed that the father of an old college buddy, Rob, had been murdered in cold blood the previous night. The crime was most certainly not random. On numerous occasions, the teenage assailant had received money, food, and unsolicited counsel from Rob's dad.

That night he did not come for food, money, or counsel. Moments after answering the door, Rob senior was choked to death, and his car stolen by this young man (if we can use that title).

My friend's Christmas letter arrived approximately three months later. The tone was surprisingly calm, very matter of fact. Below is an excerpt:

"I got a newer car this year so I can be a character witness at the trial for the murder of Dad next February. I did a Go Fund Me to help with payments . . . I've named the car JUSTICE, as I hope that's what our family gets this next year."

Justice. Every human being desires it, every human being deserves it, and all of us in one way or another demand it. Justice is like oxygen, gravity, or sleep. Rarely is it considered until someone discovers that it is missing. Justice is quiet, hidden, the invisible framework behind every relationship, every conversation, every transaction, every negotiation. It is absolutely necessary for the survival of society.

When you wait too long for your meal at your favorite restaurant, when your car is vandalized, the cashier rings up the wrong price on your peanut butter, you are snubbed by a co-worker, your spouse cheats on you, someone less qualified receives your promotion, you're robbed at gunpoint, your child lies to your face, your employer dismisses you for your religious convictions, this virtually imperceptible thing we call justice is suddenly front and center.

Justice is expected. We expect others to act with justice and others expect us to be just.

St. Thomas Aquinas tells us, "The luster of all virtues appears above all in justice"[3]; "Justice is every virtue"; "Justice is most resplendent of all the virtues." And as St. Augustine says, "Justice pervades all of the virtues."[4] In other words, justice is a big deal.

Remember that virtue is God's power, or rather, God's power is virtue. If we desire God's power, that is, the ability to terrify demons and send the devil away with his tail between his legs, we need justice and to be just. Why? Because to be powerful is to exercise virtue and **the foundation of every virtue is justice**.[5] Without justice one cannot be virtuous, and without virtue we cannot be powerful. Justice is the **supreme virtue**,[6] and therefore it gives us supreme power.

It is not an accident that the first attribute used to describe St. Joseph in Matthew's Gospel is that he was a "just man" (see Mt 1:19). This virtue is listed first because it is foundational to Joseph's character and to ours. To be named or given the title "just man" was the highest honor for a Jew. As St. Thomas says, "The virtue of justice gives its name to a good man."[7] According to St. Matthew, and divine revelation, St. Joseph was among the best of men.

But let's be clear from the start: if we misunderstand what justice really is, we can rapidly become most unjust. Even today, in modern twenty-first-century America, among so-called self-proclaimed "good Christians," there exist some very misguided notions of justice. Considering this, it is vital that we understand what justice is, why it is essential, and how we can embrace this virtue in our common, everyday lives.

Our Lord commands us, "Unless your justice abound more than the scribes and the Pharisees, you will not enter the kingdom of heaven" (Mt 5:20). These words should cause us to pause. Initially Christ's words most likely instilled alarm and a sense of hopelessness in the minds of His captive audiences, primarily comprised of Jews. How could anyone be holier than the scribes who knew the Law inside and out, and the Pharisees who have committed their lives to living the Law completely?

The scribes and the Pharisees were hailed and perceived by their Jewish kinsman as the most holy among the Israelites. They spent their lives studying, teaching, and obeying Mitzvot, the 613 commandments contained in the Torah (also known as the Law of Moses).

To obey all 613 commandments demanded continual focus and concentration, and very few people, due to the demands of life, could adequately apply themselves to this cause; and because of this most Jews could not operate at the level of a scribe or a Pharisee.

The word "Pharisee" means "separated" or "separated one." The Pharisee believed that if he separated himself, not only from the unclean gentile, but also from the common Jews who struggled at fulfilling the prescriptions of the Law perfectly, and he lived a life of righteousness, the Messiah would come and redeem Israel.

"Righteousness," or "justice" in the Hebrew *tsadeq*, was understood by the Jews as living in accordance with the Law, being innocent of charge, and seeking God above all. This idea of justice eventually became perverted, reducing religion to the fulfillment of prescribed rules, regulations, and disciplines, often at the neglect of being charitable to other human beings. This dynamic had proliferated into Judaism so greatly that it was a continually recurring theme in Jesus' teachings.

For example, in His parable about the Good Samaritan, Jesus tells of a "man who fell in with robbers, who after stripping him and beating him, went away, leaving him half-dead . . . A certain priest was going down the same way, and when he saw him, he passed by. And likewise a Levite who when he was near the place saw him, passed by. But a certain Samaritan as he journeyed came upon him, and seeing him, was moved with compassion. And he went up to him and bound up his wounds, pouring on oil and wine" (Lk 10:30–34).

The priest and the Levite were among the most respected Jews. A Levite was a member of the tribe of Levi, whose role was to assist the priests in worship in the Jewish temple. Justice according to the Levite and priest is synonymous with obeying the Law of Moses meticulously. Both the Levite and the priest would have been highly concerned about disobeying the Law that stated if any man touches a dead body, he was unclean for seven days (Num 19:11).

In addition to this, there was the possibility that the man half-dead was a gentile or could have been touched by a gentile during the beating, rendering him unclean. Again, both the Levite and the priest chose not to touch the victim to avoid becoming unclean and losing their turn to serve in the temple.

So what is the point that Jesus is trying to make with this parable? One cannot be just in God's sight by neglecting one's neighbor. *Personal transformation must always lead to and include relational transformation.* Our love of God should always lead to and include love of neighbor. If we love God but do not love our neighbor, then we are not actually loving God.

God doesn't share himself with us for us to keep Him to ourselves. He must be shared. If religion is reduced to personal holiness it eventually becomes self-righteous, self-focused, just "me and God" religion. If justice is just "me and God," then it is actually "just me," because God wants it to be "we and God." This is precisely why our Lord taught us to address God beginning with the word "Our." God is "Our Father." He's not just my Father, or your Father, but *our* Father. We may be tempted to focus on our own prayer life, our own personal spiritual practices, and our own sacrifices, while neglecting to wish and will the good of another.

Justice is a highly complex topic, one that philosophers and theologians have discoursed on at length throughout the centuries. But for the sake of simplicity we are going to take a stab at explaining justice for three reasons: to become virtuous, to conquer evil, to free ourselves from slavery to Satan. Our vantage point for applying justice will not be for political, legal, or sociological purposes, but for spiritual growth. Our goal is to understand justice in a way that allows us to move beyond being the legalist Pharisee who reduces a relationship with God and religion to the strict fulfillment of the law, and rather to learn how to be *just* like St. Joseph.

Traditionally, justice has two forms: particular and general.[8] Particular justice is essentially what one owes another. It is related to a particular person and a particular situation. General justice is being just in a way that improves oneself, and that improvement eventually has a general, positive effect on society. Though these distinctions are essential, for our purposes we will discuss justice as being either ordinary or extraordinary.

First, ordinary justice is what is demanded of *all* people in the most common circumstances of life. For example, your car is serviced at the local auto repair shop. Justice demands that you pay the auto shop the amount due for the service rendered. It would be a grave injustice, in fact stealing, if you did not pay the exact amount. To give another person his due is known as *ordinary* justice.[9] Society cannot properly operate or function fairly without ordinary justice.

Ordinary justice is also rendered when someone commits a crime. Justice demands that the person who committed the crime "pay."

Now, ordinary justice does not necessarily determine holiness, but nevertheless it is the indispensable foundation for it. This is important because human beings are tempted to fulfill legal prescriptions of religion to the letter of the law and to believe that is the essence of holiness. The priest and the Levite both succumbed to that temptation . . . and both were wrong. On the other hand, there are those who neglect religious laws, doctrines, and disciplines for the sake of creating a better society. An example of this would be those who are fearful of overpopulation and propagate the aborting of infants to ensure the sustainability of the earth's resources. This is also a grave distortion of true justice.

If you and I are to become like St. Joseph, a terror of demons, it is imperative that we not only express ordinary justice but are willing to give justice to God in a way that supremely honors him. Given that God has created us in His image and likeness and has given us every good gift, we are indebted to Him. In addition to this, since other human beings are also created in His image and likeness, we are also, in a certain sense, indebted to God in our neighbor. So we owe our neighbor something beyond ordinary justice.

This type of justice, which we will call extraordinary, moves beyond giving only exactly what is due to another. Extraordinary justice wishes and wills the good of the other by doing something for the sake of their own good, something that is beyond "not doing wrong."[10]

In other words, justice can have three levels: first ordinary justice, which is giving to a person exactly what is owed—including punishment for a crime or an infraction; second, wishing the good of another beyond what they are technically owed; and third, the ultimate form of extraordinary justice, which honors the presence of God in another by giving them love, respect, and honor for the purpose of them experiencing God and achieving their ultimate end, which is happiness in God.

To move beyond an exacting, legalistic form of justice to a generous, virtuous form of justice that wills the good of another demands a mind shift. Perhaps an example will help us understand this concept.

Recently, my wife and I met an old friend and his wife at a restaurant for dinner. Our waitress was wonderful. She had memorized the menus, recited the specials from memory, promptly anticipated our needs, was jovial and kind without being too intrusive . . . but she avoided making eye contact. She looked past us or over us when talking to us. It was unsettling. Her behavior seemed to indicate that she suffered from personal insecurity.

Ordinary justice demanded that she be tipped 20 percent of the dinner's total cost. To pay that would be giving her the exact amount owed to her. But I felt inclined to give her more, not just monetarily, but personally—to give her due, to honor her in such a way that upheld her dignity and could help to offset whatever insecurity plagued her.

Before we left, I found her name on our receipt. I thought that by addressing her with her name she might feel acknowledged as a unique person with a real identity. I wanted her to know that I knew she was more than a waitress, but a person who had gifts to share with the world.

"Abbey," I said, "thank you for being an excellent waitress." Suddenly our eyes connected. I continued. "You are so talented. You are so good with people, at anticipating our needs." Our eyes remained locked on the other's. "You made our evening very special. I don't know what your calling is in life, but I have a feeling it has something to do with working in the service industry, making people happy. Thank you for being you." She remained motionless as her eyes welled up with tears. She began to wave her hand over her face. "I'm heating up," she said. "That is the nicest thing someone has said to me . . . You made my night."

God prompted me to move beyond giving her exactly what was owed to her monetarily. I was inspired to wish good for her. But wishing, or praying for her, didn't seem enough. I felt compelled to act, and intentionally will her good by doing good to her. In that moment, I sensed that I was honoring God within her, and consequently honoring her. My hope is that she would taste the goodness of God, if even for a moment, and realize that she was made for Him.

The purpose of this example is not to pat myself on the back, but to demonstrate that God inspires us to move beyond the minimal requirements of the law that demands giving someone their exact due, to willing the good of the other actively, positively. This kind of justice has the power to vanquish the devil. To pay for dinner and to tip Abbey was not extraordinary justice—because the law and cultural norms demand it, it is therefore ordinary. There is nothing special about it. But to move beyond the letter of the law is an extraordinary form of justice that is imbued with charity. *The justice of a saint moves beyond not doing wrong to a person, but rather focusing on willing the other's good.*

We cannot be extraordinarily just without first being just in ordinary ways. Nevertheless, ordinary justice should condition us to practice extraordinary justice.

Now, there exists a tension, and a real one at that, in finding the balance between scrupulously feeling the urge to apply extraordinary justice to the eight billion people on planet Earth and rendering people their exact due and nothing more. To avoid either mistake, we can apply what my friend Joe calls the rule of relational proximity.

The rule of relational proximity can be explained this way: the closer the person is in relationship to us, the greater the responsibility we have to exercise extraordinary justice to do something good for the person's own sake rather than making sure that we are giving them the minimum due and nothing more.

Parents have a closer proximity to their children than to homeless children in a third-world country. Does this mean that they ignore the children in a third-world country? Not necessarily. But it also does not mean that they ignore their own children's needs for the purpose of helping human beings in impoverished nations.

The range of relational proximity from closest to furthest begins with family, then to friends, then to associates, to acquaintances, and finally to people that we encounter casually on the streets, at the bus stop, or at the store.

We should make the effort to intentionally make eye contact with our spouse, speak and listen respectfully to our spouse and children, anticipate their needs and serve them as though we were serving Christ. By doing so, we exercise responsibility for those in closest proximity to us. This is just.

Yet we ought to greet warmly the person standing next to us at the bus stop or in the grocery line, without scrupulously feeling compelled to purchase their groceries and shine their shoes.

The key is prudence. We must use our intellect and our experience to know when to exercise extraordinary justice and to know when ordinary justice is demanded. It is imperative that we ask God to challenge us in this area lest we systematically become indifferent to other's needs. Which brings us to an important point: people's authentic needs are intrinsically linked to a right that is owed to them.

Often, justice is confined to the sphere of being wronged. We tend to think of justice only when we are violated. Justice is enacted to punish a crime or to obtain retribution for a wrong inflicted. But justice doesn't only exist to right a wrong; rather, it is a right. Justice has less to do with something wrong as it has to do with people's rights.

The word "justice" comes from the Latin root word *jus*, which is defined as a right that is owed to someone. This means that justice is giving another person their due. We have heard someone say, "I don't owe anyone anything." But is that true? Everyone owes someone something, because that someone, no matter who they are, is made in the image and likeness of God.

The actual meaning of justice is "using one's will to render to another his due, perpetually."[11] Which raises another question: what is another's due? What exactly do we owe to others? That is the essence of the question to which our Lord responded with the parable of the Good Samaritan—"Who is my neighbor?" In other words, "Who do I owe justice to?"

Every person has the right to pursue happiness and to be happy, and to pursue the ultimate Good, which is God. For that reason, every person should be given respect, honor, and charity in a way that inspires them to desire God.

The most basic right owed to human beings is to be known and to be loved by another.[12] Which presents a tremendous challenge: one can only know and love another, and be loved and known by another, in a social context; in other words, in a relationship. The virtue of justice is *always* required of those who relate to one another.[13] Every single person, unless they are a cloistered hermit, is required to exercise the virtue of justice every day. And even the hermit must be just by praying and sacrificing for others.

Justice is *only* possible in a relationship.[14] Again, this indicates that we cannot be the Pharisee, the separatist, and expect to have power over the devil. Every action, transaction, communication between two human beings involves justice. *No other virtue is this pervasive.* Giving the other person eye contact, listening to the other person without interrupting, controlling your anger and talking kindly and calmly with another, are all actions that are founded upon justice—what we owe the other person. No other virtue is that foundational and fundamental.

For example, a person can be temperate, eat and drink less—by himself. A person can persevere, express the virtue of fortitude—by herself. I can be prudent and exercise the virtue of wisdom (like writing this book, I hope)—by myself.

But justice is always a virtue that is expressed and exercised between two or more human beings. It is a right owed to one person from another person. Which raises a tangential but important point: the term "social justice" is an accurate term but has been hijacked by progressives who have a socialist agenda. Those who use the term *social justice* to guilt and control people by demanding that they owe their lives to the state at the neglect of the person's most fundamental rights, such as life, freedom of religion, and liberty, are the misusing and misunderstanding social justice.

Justice is by its very nature social and is the foundation of every secure and lasting relationship. It is an injustice to elevate issues such as environmentalism, immigration, and giving sustenance to the less fortunate while minimizing the justice demanded in every social relationship, whether it be marital, familial, or work-related. In fact, a just society is founded upon upholding the sanctity of heterosexual marriage, the traditional family, and freedom of religion. The key factor in all of these relationships is that justice respects and defends the dignity of human life at its very foundation. Justice mandates that every person is given the right to life, and the right to worship God, because life is from God and for God.

When we say that helping the less fortunate is a truer form of social justice, we pit that type of justice against the protection of the most basic and essential types of justice. We become conditioned to look upon the right to life, or the right to religious freedom, or service to one's family members through one's vocation as a lower class of justice compared to external corporal works of mercy.

So often those who defend the unborn are viewed as single-issue voters. They are often misunderstood as being anti-social justice or promoting social injustice. Yet, Isaiah said, ". . . share your food with the hungry and provide the poor wanderer with shelter—when you see the naked, clothe them, and not to turn away from your own flesh and blood" (Isa 58:7). In other words, true justice begins at home. Society goes by way of the family. When we are just at home, society becomes more just. Justice begins with those to whom we are closest.

When our Lord said, "Unless your justice abound more than the scribes and Pharisees, you cannot enter the kingdom of heaven" (Mt 5:20), He meant it. The scribes and the Pharisees made the mistake of believing that religion can be reduced to strict justice—to the fulfillment of legal prescriptions. They made the error of believing they could prance past a man half-dead on the side of the road, leaving him to die a slow, agonizing death, and still have rich communion with God later that day. Do you see the incompatibility of the two actions? They are completely irreconcilable. Indeed, how can you love the God you cannot see, if you do not love the brother or sister that you have seen (see 1 Jn 4:20). Our justice must surpass this kind of pharisaical religion.

Our justice surpasses the scribe and the Pharisee when we realize that the perfect fulfillment of prescribed religious disciplines and doctrines doesn't make a person holy—it is only the beginning. Why? Because anyone can obey rules and regulations and exercise spiritual disciplines and yet ignore their neighbor's need.

St. Thomas Aquinas tells us, "It is love of God and love of neighbor which pervades all virtues,"[15] and St. Augustine says, "Justice pervades all of the virtues."[16] So love of neighbor and love of God *is* justice—and this justice is found in *every* virtue—and therefore justice should be evident and manifest in *all* of our relationships.

And this is why St. Joseph is a just man. The Sacred Scripture says that after discovering Mary, his wife, pregnant without his cooperation, "Joseph, being a just man, decided to put her away privately" (Mt 1:19).

But there's a difficulty. According to the Law of Moses, a woman discovered pregnant before the second stage of Jewish marriage (the solemnization) would be executed by stoning.

To be just according to the Jew was to fulfill the Law perfectly. Therefore it would seem that if Joseph were truly a just man he would have submitted obediently to the Law's demands and had Mary executed.[17] But Scripture says that "Joseph decided to put Mary away privately." How could he be a "just man?"

There is no doubt that Joseph knew Mary well. He admired her dignity, her beauty, her holiness, and her purity. Because of these attributes he fell in love with her and because of this knowledge he could not accept the idea that Mary had committed adultery.

Joseph, being a just man, "meditated on the Law of the Lord both day and night" (Ps 1). He was well-versed in the Scriptures and was familiar with the prophecy, "A virgin shall conceive and bear a son (Isa 7:14) . . . he shall be called Wonderful, Counsellor, Mighty God, Everlasting Father, Prince of Peace (Is 9:6). Because of this knowledge, Joseph could not ignore the extreme possibility that Mary's pregnancy was of divine origin . . . But he could not prove it.

Though he believed that Mary was innocent, he was incapable of producing the evidence of Mary's innocence to the religious authorities. For Joseph, this was an extremely confounding situation. By having her executed he would have judged her unjustly. By claiming and defending her innocence he would have judged her unjustly also—because he could not know for certain that the child was of God. So how could Joseph be just?

Recall that justice cannot be reduced to being a Levite or priest who legalistically fulfills the Law while ignoring his neighbor. Justice is always accomplished in the context of a relationship. Therefore, the context in which Joseph had to express justice was his relationship with Mary. To be just was to give Mary her due of honor and respect, and to love her for *her own sake.*

Mary, like all of us, had the right to pursue happiness and the ultimate good, which is God—particularly the God-man conceived within her. Associated with this right to pursue happiness is the right to life, the protection of that life, sustenance, and the right to be known and to be loved.

Joseph was just and exercised the virtue of justice by giving Mary her due. By refusing to judge her or to allow others to pronounce judgment upon her, he could protect her life and the life within her; he could protect her innocence; he could protect her relationship with God and allow her to continue to pursue Him.

Joseph is just because he loved Mary for her own sake. "Justice disregards its own profit in order to preserve common equity."[18] He did not love her for what she could give to him, but for who she was. Joseph concluded that the best way to protect Mary and the child within her was to put her away privately—so that she could be hidden with God. By doing so, St. Joseph expressed *extraordinary justice*.

If we could reduce St. Joseph's just character to one fundamental action it would be that he did not judge Mary, or subject her dignity to be judged. Joseph did not usurp God's authority to judge.

Now, it is important to qualify these statements. As Catholics it is imperative that we judge. We must judge right from wrong, good from evil, sinful actions from objectively good moral actions. This is exercising the virtue of prudence. God commands us to judge in this way.

But we can take this type of judging too far by judging the soul of another individual. For example, a person could endorse a presidential candidate who advocates for maintaining the legalization of abortion and supporting abortions with government funding. Abortion is evil. Funding abortion is evil. But we take it too far when we judge the person who is an advocate of that candidate, or the candidate himself, as evil. We simply cannot make that judgment, for we are not God. God judges the heart (see 2 Sam 2:15). We do not have that right or capability. We are to judge actions without judging the soul of the one acting.

Joseph could not have been a just man if he judged Mary—that would have been unjust. Rather than judging Mary, he left the judgment to the Eternal Judge to sort out. Joseph owed Mary that right. And he was humble enough to know that. That is why he is just.

How does this apply to us?

If we want to embody and express the power of God and not allow the devil to have any power over us, it is imperative that we be just like Joseph (pun intended).

So often we play God. We establish ourselves as the supreme judge of others' motives and character. We categorize people as good, bad, holy, evil, and in doing so we expose people's failures, faults, and sins to the world, believing that we are protecting the public good.

We fail to acknowledge that people have the right to get right with God, and that God alone has the right to judge their heart and their motives. We overlook the fact that people who sin have the right to be known and to be loved, and it is being known and loved that can draw them from darkness into light. Often it is because we subconsciously feel unknown and unloved that we disregard other's rights to be known and to be loved. Wounded people wound people.

Frequently, the self-righteous carry within themselves the wound of feeling unloved, unknown, disrespected. They believe that by appearing perfect they will earn the respect and favor of others. They become experts at being right by proving that others are wrong. Their self-righteousness becomes pronounced when they expose other's sinfulness.

Social media has its advantages and benefits. Although justice is expressed socially, social media does not often express justice. Too often, we use social media as a virtual bulletproof shield and grenade launcher simultaneously. From behind that shield, distanced by miles of copper cable lines and satellite feeds, we launch our bombs of detraction, defamation that demoralizes and destroys other people's reputations and character.

Recently, I witnessed a very prominent Catholic evangelist verbally trash the character of a prominent Catholic priest, accusing him of leading the flock astray. Though the priest had led thousands upon thousands to conversion, this verbal assault spurred a virtual revolt against him, wreaking havoc on all of his social media platforms.

The Catholic evangelist judged the motives of the priest and deemed him to be a wolf in sheep's clothing. But it wasn't enough for him to make that judgment and keep it to himself. It burned and seethed within until it simmered and boiled over, and he began to compel and convince others to feel the same. The sinner who forgets that he is a sinner and judges another, doesn't realize that his act of judgment proves that he is a worse kind of sinner—for as the saying goes, "It takes one to know one." The moment that a person deems another person unworthy to be a child of God, he has deemed himself unworthy of being one of God's children.

On this matter our Lord speaks clearly and emphatically: "Stop judging and you will not be judged. Stop condemning and you will not be condemned" (Lk 6:36–38). Let's pause there. What is the implication? If you judge you will be judged. If you condemn you will be condemned. This is serious. Jesus is telling us that we will reap what we sow, both in this life and in the next.

Mother Teresa said, "If all you do is judge, you have no time to love." We must be careful. Our self-righteousness can convince us that we are right and have the right to expose everyone else's wrong. There are many people who may be right but express it in the wrong way.

Let's continue with our Lord's words: "Forgive and you will be forgiven." This is a positive command: go forth and be merciful. Forgive. It moves beyond simply *not* making rash judgments about people's character and motivations, which is ordinary justice. It summons us to be Christ and make Christ known in this world of hatred and indifference by forgiving, which is extraordinary justice.

Now you might be thinking that's all well and good, but there are evil people in this world, criminals who commit heinous crimes and are a real threat to society. Justice demands that such individuals be punished and incarcerated. That is true. And yet, we as Christians are called by God not only to apply ordinary justice (in this case by means of punishment), but also to apply extraordinary justice to the worst of criminals. After all, our Lord did command us to visit those who are in prison. Perhaps an example will help explain how we can integrate and apply both ordinary and extraordinary justice in our lives.

Last year I was on the last leg of my trip home from meetings out East. A middle-aged woman sat in the seat next me. We greeted each other and she promptly put in her headphones, which is like saying, "Leave me alone, I need to chill."

Over the course of the flight she began to talk to me. Initially our conversation consisted of superfluous niceties. It wasn't until after I asked her why she traveled so often that she began to reveal her life story.

As long as she, Mandy, could remember, her dad was a kingpin drug dealer. As a little girl as young as four, her dad would have her weigh the drugs. As a teenager she began doing interstate drug runs, while dealing and doing. She eventually became an addict. Though she had evaded police authorities over the years, she was arrested for drug possession and drug trafficking in her mid-thirties.

As the police officer cuffed her, she cold-cocked him and spit in his face. She was tried and found guilty of multiple felonies—including assaulting a police officer—and incurred a hefty prison sentence. Ordinary justice was rightly applied to Mandy.

While she was in prison, the judge who convicted her asked to see her. Initially, she refused. But eventually she became lonely, and one day, in a moment of weakness, she allowed him to visit her.

The visits continued, and over the course of many meetings they became friends. During one of their visits, Mandy asked the judge why he had taken an interest in her. He said that he was just like her. She laughed. To which he responded, "I'm serious . . . I'm a sinner who needs a Savior."

This judge embodied a very important truth: all men sin and are deprived of God's glory (see Rom 3:23), and therefore each and every one of us need a Savior. His ability to see himself in Mandy allowed her to see herself in him. Because he could see his sin in her, she could see her redemption in him; and because of him, that day she surrendered her life to Jesus Christ.

Mandy finished her story by saying that the day she was paroled not one member of her family or any of her old drug friends came to the prison to greet her. There were, however, two people who were present to welcome her with open arms: the judge and the officer she had cold-cocked . . . He had been praying for her during her imprisonment. This is an example of extraordinary justice.

Rarely is a person converted from conviction and condemnation. Yet that conviction serves as a first step that is intended to awaken the person to their grave guilt, which can lead them to repentance. When that conviction is built upon with love from a non-condemning individual, a person can experience conversion to Christ. Condemnation rarely converts. Almost always a person is converted by love. Paraphrasing St. Augustine, the person you judge good may end up damned, and those you judge damned may end up good.

To be just is to be powerful. Though the judge was powerful in giving Mandy her just sentence, he expressed even greater power by bringing Christ to her.

It is important to make a qualification. Every person is owed the right to pursue happiness, which ultimately can only be found in God. But sin is not happiness, nor the path to it. So, no person has the right to sin, nor does anyone have the right to give that person the right to sin. That is injustice. The judge refused to grant Mandy the right to continue sinning; but he also gave her the dignity and respect that is due to a person made in the image and likeness of God. There is power in love of neighbor. There is power in that kind of justice.

So what about you and me? How do we express justice? The first step is to examine our relationships, because that is the context of justice—always. Ask yourself about those relationships. For example: is there someone to whom I owe a return call? When we postpone calling or texting a person back it is often because we think they aren't all that important, which means that we are not treating them justly. We owe them the call.

Is there someone, perhaps a relative, that you have put off visiting? They are owed the right to be loved and to be known. Are you slow in paying back a loan or returning something you borrowed from a friend? When we delay payback, we are not giving that person their due. Do you belittle your children, demean your spouse? Do you become jealous or envious of friends? Do you lose your patience with co-workers or clients?

It may be difficult to see, but in all of the cases listed we are judging the other person. Because when we act in this way, we are making a statement that we are more important than they are, which means that we have judged them to be less, and therefore we give them less.

Our Lord ends with these words, "For the measure with which you measure will in return be measured out to you" (Mt 7:2). How does our Lord Jesus measure? With the perfect forgiveness of Christ, who asked of His Father, while enduring the torments inflicted by His executioners, "Father, forgive them for they know not what they do" (Lk 23:34).

Our Lord understands that we really don't understand why we sin, why we are so selfish, why we continue to hurt the people around us, and that is one of the reasons why He is patient with us. Yet this gift of patience demands that we owe others our patience. For Our Lord says in His parable of the wicked servant, "Should not you have had mercy on your fellow servant, as I had mercy on you?" (Mt 18:33). Considering what God has done for us, we can never limit justice to merely *not doing wrong* to another or to giving them the minimum due. Rather, we must give to others the very right that God in His rich mercy has given to us: to experience and embrace His mercy. God applied the condemnation caused by our sins to His Son. Jesus received the justice that should have been measured out to us. He applies His mercy to us. But there is a condition: we must be merciful to others as He has been merciful to us. For if we do not receive and give His mercy, we will, in the end, receive His justice.

Our Lord loves you because He sees Himself in you. God loves all because He sees Himself in all. That is true justice: to see the image of perfection in imperfect beings, and to give them the respect that God gives them.

When you respond to God's grace and see His perfect image in the imperfect people around you, and even within yourself, then you will begin to "be perfect as your heavenly Father is perfect . . . who maketh the sun to rise upon the good, and bad, and raineth upon the just and the unjust (Mt 5:45). This is just power, and the power of the just.

CHAPTER 3

Secret Power

Prestige. Prominence. Recognition. Honor. At some level, each human person desires to be noticed and known for the good that they do, that they are. Such notoriety is like sugar—once you taste it, you crave more, and obtaining more, your craving is not satiated, but rather increased. If you don't believe me, spend a little time on any of your favorite social media platforms. Many people will do nearly anything to obtain the attention they desire.

It seems natural. We all want to be important, special—even great. These desires in themselves are innate to the human person. However, if they become the driving force behind our motivations, we will eventually become entangled in depression, resentment, anxiety, comparisons, and envy—all of which make for a miserable existence.

Recently, I read an article titled "Negativity Is a Drug, and We're Hooked."[19]

The author of the article vented his frustration, describing how "the stuff that's positive and motivating and helps us to live better, more virtuous lives" is overlooked, "but the minute someone drops a nasty negative, outrageous story in front of us, we swarm like flies."

It continued, "We've all been wired to seek out negativity. The old newspaper adage, 'If it bleeds, it leads,' isn't just a cliché." . . . "But it's hard not to think of yourself as a drug dealer sometimes, when you publish stories that can be described this way. People are addicted, and you wonder if you're feeding it. Worse, you wonder if you're doing it because traffic is how you pay the bills."

It is commendable that this blogger is vulnerable enough to reveal his sore dilemma, but he may not be diagnosing the root of his problem. Perhaps a more revealing and indicting title for the article would have been *"Vainglory* Is a Drug, and We're Hooked."

It is easy to miss this. We blame scandal, negativity, alarmism, and sensationalism as the problem, and though people crave such negativity, those who provide it crave something more egregious and fatal. It is vainglory, and it is this base desire for vainglory that keeps the sensationalistic negativity ball rolling.

The truth is that to a greater or lesser degree, this grave temptation bites and chews at all of us. If I didn't have to battle against it, and at times suffer personal losses because of it, I couldn't write about it. Often, I feel like a marionette, a puppet attached to the strings of human respect, vain ambition, envy, resentment, vainglory, and worst of all, the steel cable of pride, all of which are connected to a crossbar held in the controlling grip of the devil himself.

The experience is nearly automatic, a sick, perverted kind of normal. I set myself in motion to accomplish a noble task without realizing that my motivation is not completely sincere. If I'm honest with myself, I am not always, or consistently, altruistic. I am seeking something else. Something unhealthy. What desire is driving me?

I desire glory. You desire glory. And there is nothing inherently wrong with desiring glory. In fact, as Catholics we believe that the desire for glory is not a sin,[20] but a wholesome and necessary desire.

Glory, according to St. Augustine, is clarity: someone's good that is clearly seen.[21] Glory occurs when something bodily or spiritual is appealing and attractive.[22]

Goodness reflects glory, and glory is good. It is important that we believe and understand this, lest we condemn something that is good as being bad. Good Catholics, who seriously pursue holiness, often commit this mistake.

For example, alcohol can lead to alcoholism; therefore alcohol is bad (even though Christ transformed water not into a cheap common wine, but into the best wine). Pleasure can condition someone to become hedonistic, therefore anything pleasurable must be suppressed (though God created things like sexual intercourse to be pleasurable). Do you see the problem with thinking this way? We often throw out the baby, which is good, with the bathwater, which has become dirty, because we too closely associate the dirt, the sin, with the virtue, the gift.

Glory, and the desire for glory, is a great good because glory is relative to goodness. St. Thomas Aquinas tells us that it is not a sin to acknowledge or approve our own goodness. Rather, God requires it of us.[23]

To deny your own goodness is to reject the God who created you good. I believe that this is why so many potentially good Catholics become embittered: they suppress their own glory, deeming it to be sinful, and then seeing glory in others they fall prey to jealousy, envy, resentment, and the like.

To acknowledge your goodness and thank God for it is to glorify the God who shares His glory with you. Indeed, as St. Paul says, "We have received the Spirit of God that we may know the things given to us by God" (see 1 Cor 2:12). God the Holy Spirit reminds us that God has shared with us His glory, and that we are to rejoice and partake in this gift.

We are to "seek glory and honor and incorruption, eternal life" (Rom 2:7), and "we are called by the gospel, to the obtaining of the glory of our Lord Jesus Christ" (2 Thes 2:14). So what's the problem? How can desiring glory be a bad thing? Desiring glory is *not* the problem. Succumbing to vainglory is. The key is to identify how the goodness of glory becomes tarnished by vanity.

St. Thomas tells us that there are three ways that glory becomes tainted and perverted. First, glory becomes tainted if we seek it in perishable things. For example: a person purchases a vehicle not for the practical purposes that a vehicle offers, but to exalt his own image and reputation. We don't realize this, but we do this type of thing consistently. Often, we purchase clothing that is immodest and accentuates certain parts of our glorious bodies for the purpose of revealing and reveling in our physical glory. One of the reasons we have difficulty perceiving this is because almost the entire commercial industry is based on this principle. It is not a sin to have nice cars or nice clothes. But when we crave the glory that these perishable things can afford, it becomes sinful.

Second, glory becomes vain when we seek glory from human beings. Threaded throughout the Gospels is the recurring theme of the Pharisees who love the seats of honor in the synagogues (see Lk 11:43; Mt 23:6), who pray in the marketplaces to be seen by others (see Mt 6:5), who blow a horn before giving their offerings (see Mt 6:2), who widen their phylacteries and lengthen their tassels (Mt 23:5); who perform all their works to be seen by men (see Mt 23:5). Why do they do such things? More important, why does Jesus condemn such practices? Because they are literally perform-ing these actions to acquire honors, accolades, prestige, and respect from men.

Third, glory becomes perverted when a man claims that the glory he has received, or the lion's share of it, is exclusive-ly his own, rather than coming from God and for God, and used for the purpose of directing others to God.

For example, an artist who creates a masterpiece, when lauded and praised, does not reference God, or give any credit to God, for his work. We might say, of course he shouldn't because he is the one who created it. But did not God give him the talent, the substrate, the tools, the people who educated him in the craft, and on and on and on?

Of the three perversions of glory, this is the most malicious because it attempts to steal or usurp God's glory, claiming it as our own. Our goodness, instead of leading people to God, leads people to us, conditioning them to regard us as god.

Another simpler way to determine clearly whether we are perverting glory into vainglory is to ask, "What is my inten-tion?" Recall that motivations matter. Is my intention to glo-rify God and to be an expression of God's glory, and to help others experience God? To help others to "see the good that we do and give glory to God" (Mt 5:16)?

Or is our intention to obtain glory as our ultimate goal—even if we have to use God to obtain it? There are people who use God to possess glory, and there are others who are possessed by God to share His glory. Which of the two are you? Which do you want to be?

So often we forget that the glory we have is not actually our own. It is a gift from God. St. Paul asks, "What do you have that you have not received and if you have received, why do you glory as though you did not receive it?" (1 Cor 4:7).

Glory is from God and is a reward for those who glorify God. Glorify God and He cannot help but to glorify you—it is a supernatural law. Glory becomes vainglory, even sinful, when our desire for human glory, earthly prestige, and praise and honor from others replaces our desire to glorify God with our goodness.

This poses a great challenge for us. We have been conditioned to believe that glory is contingent on being seen and approved by men. Consequently we conclude that if we are not honored by men, we are not men of honor. But St. Thomas assures us that perfection consists in knowing oneself—but not that a man should be known by others.[24] What a relief!

My perfection, your perfection, our glory does not depend on others knowing us, acknowledging us, or praising us; it only depends on us knowing ourselves, being known by God, and knowing the True God, and becoming who God has destined us to be.

St. Joseph wasn't popular, famous, or known and acknowledged by men. In fact, not one word of Joseph's is recorded in Sacred Scripture. Further, only on one occasion in the Gospels did a person specifically reference Joseph, albeit tangentially, to Christ: "Is this not the carpenter's Son" (Mt 13:55). In other words, "Jesus is not a big deal. He is only the son of that poor, obscure carpenter." Additionally, we have no record of any piece of Joseph's craftsmanship or of any mighty deeds that he may have accomplished. No, St. Joseph was not renowned in his lifetime.

What we do have record of is that after discovering the Blessed Virgin Mary, his wife, pregnant without his cooperation, St. Matthew tells us that "Joseph was minded to put Mary away privately" (Mt 1:19). The Greek word for privately is *lathra*, which means *secret*. What this indicates is that St. Joseph fulfilled God's will in a hidden, secret way.

This is confirmed by the fact that when Herod sought to destroy the child Jesus and His Mother, "Joseph arose and took the child and his mother *by night* and withdrew to Egypt" (Mt 2:14). St. Joseph is a symbol of the human father who succeeds in shrouding and saving the mother and child, the family, by embracing the dark night, the secret hidden life of fatherhood. This dark night consists of the humiliating and harsh reality of surrendering desire for fame, fortune, popularity, and prestige in exchange for obedience to God and His glory.

It should be noted that Herod, a symbol of the devil, is unable to destroy the child and His mother because of the secrecy of St. Joseph. St. Joseph is Terror of Demons and most powerful because his way is *lathra*, secret. The secret man is not loud and proud. The secret man is determined to glorify God. He knows that his purpose is to know God and be known by God, rather than to be noticed by men and renowned among men. Such a man avoids the snares of the devil and snatches souls from the snares of the devil.

So many of us are powerless over the devil because our intentions and motivations are not meant to be secret, but to bring attention to ourselves for the sake of our own self-exaltation.

"Why do you love vanity?" God asks (see Ps 4: 3), for "even the love of praise is sinful" (St. Augustine). "Vainglory enters secretly, and robs us insensibly, of all our inward possessions" (St. John Chrysostom), therefore we must "be aware of the desire for glory since it enslaves the mind."[25]

Nevertheless, we plunge headfirst into the vast black ocean of human honor, hoping to drink our fill because we "love the glory of men more than the glory of God" (Jn 12:43).

What keeps us from accepting and imitating Joseph's way of secrecy? There appear to be three fundamental reasons why we don't embrace the hidden way of St. Joseph. First, we misunderstand what secrecy is. We think that to be hidden means that we hide our good or deny the good that God is doing through us. This is not Joseph's way of secrecy. If we purposefully suppress our goodness, we are demonstrating false humility, which is a form of pride. By denying or suppressing the glory of our goodness we deny the goodness and glory of God in us. St. Thomas Aquinas said, *humilitas est veritas*, humility is truth. We simply need to be true to God and his goodness in us. My friend Greg, who stands at a booming six foot three and looks like a Greek god, once said to me, "Schadt, I can't hide the fact that I am big and strong any more than you can hide your faith."

Truth is like light. When light enters darkness, the darkness flees. Light cannot be overcome by darkness unless a person purposefully snuffs it out. Extinguishing the light of your goodness is satanic. It would be like my friend Greg amputating his legs to purposefully diminish his stature. The devil desires that you cover up the goodness of God that lives in you. The devil knows that if you become a living manifestation and revelation of God's glory, you will do tremendous damage to his diabolical empire.

Sunlight shines naturally, and like the sun your goodness shines and shows naturally. You don't have to shove your light in people's faces. If you do, you blind them. Rather, we are to use the light given to us to reveal the path toward God. Notice the difference? If your light is directed toward you, then you are leading people to you and encouraging yourself and others to commit idolatry, making yourself a god; but by shining your light toward God, people find the path to God.

Jesus commands us, "Let your light shine before men, that they may see the glory of God" (Mt 5:16). The intention is not to make people see your glory, but to help people see the glory of God through you. Notice also that the verb Jesus uses is not *force* or *make* but *let*. Let others see your light. Don't force it.

Unfortunately, "making" people see our light has become the habit of nearly every twenty-first century human being. We plaster what we eat for breakfast on Instagram, we populate our Facebook profiles with photos from our perfect family vacations and our yoga poses in halter tops and painted-on Spanx, all for the subconscious and sometimes conscious intention of saying, "Hey, everybody, look how great my life is!" And we eclipse the glory of God.

You and I are created to be like the moon. The moon reflects the light of the sun into the darkness of night. We are to reflect the glory of the Son into hopeless hearts. But too often, we move our little moon directly in front of the sun and eclipse the very light that we are created to reflect.

You and I are to let our goodness shine for the purpose of saying, "Hey, look how awesome God is!" This goodness is always founded upon the intention to be like St. Joseph, to be secret; to do everything for the glory of God.

The second reason we don't embrace the hidden way of St. Joseph is because we misunderstand secrecy as a consequence rather than an intention. Our focus should not be on controlling the outcome: that is, whether I am noticed by men or not. God takes care of the consequence. Our job is to ensure that our intention is pure: to glorify God.

On one hand, you can try to "hide your light," but by attempting to hide your light, you will eventually extinguish it. If you don't use a muscle it atrophies. If you don't use your money, you may save it, but over the course of time its value decreases. The way to increase money is to invest it. The way to build muscles mass is to exercise your muscles. The way to increase your light is to use it, and by using it, it becomes impossible to hide because it increases.

On the other hand, we can attempt to make others see our light. Like a salesman who seeks out customers, we set out with the purpose of showing people our goodness, with the hidden purpose of obtaining the praises of men. You don't have to show anything. If you are good your goodness will be manifest.

Often, we avoid embracing the hidden life because we are afraid that we will become forgotten, unimportant, and unneeded. It is imperative that we overcome this fear. Our Lord promised, "There is nothing hidden that will not be revealed" (Lk 8:17). Without any doing of his own, St. Joseph's hidden life is becoming increasingly well known. In other words, the intention to be secret like St. Joseph is yours; the consequential effect and reality is God's. St. Joseph deliberately chose to act secretly, without pomp. Yet, God chose to reveal His glory through him.

The third reason we avoid a life of secrecy is because we do not adequately comprehend the reward God has in store for those who live this way of life.

"Those who are hidden in God will not be condemned" (Ps 34). God promises that the person who is decidedly hidden will not only avoid Hell but be admitted to the eternal abode of heaven. When you pray, fast, or give alms, do it for "Your Father who is in secret and your Father who sees in secret will repay you" (Mt6:6). From this we can conclude that we who are like our Father, who is in secret, will be rewarded by this secret Father. In other words, God who is glory will share His glory with you.

St. Joseph was little known in his lifetime and yet is the most lauded, honored, and glorified husband and father of all-time. Truly what is hidden will be revealed. Glorify God and He cannot help but to glorify you.

Probing more deeply the question why we don't embrace secrecy, there is a more profound reason why we succumb to vainglory instead of true glory: We simply don't believe that God is enough.

When we doubt that God loves us, desires us, chooses us, and has created us for Him; that we may experience the love that He is and experience it for all eternity, we settle for chasing after the world's trophies and trinkets.

When we doubt that we have God's approval we succumb to seeking the approval of men. When we don't believe that we are important to God, we strive to be important to men. When we doubt that God delights in us, we scramble, scratch, and claw for any piece of affirmation, honor, and human respect that is left on the curbside with the weekly trash. We attempt to fill a soul that is made for the infinite love of God with the finite accolades of fallen, sinful human beings.

When we forget that God is our Father, we cease to be trusting sons. When we stop trusting God the Father, we will fail to be trustworthy sons; for we will succumb to usurping His glory as our own. Therefore we cannot be trusted with His glory.

Okay, so that's negative. But on the flip side, the positive side, what does it look like to be a son who trusts his Father? When our Lord Jesus was baptized, the heavens opened and the voice of the Father thundered, "You are my beloved Son, with whom I am well pleased" (Mk 1:11). These words roll over our ears like water glides over a smooth rock. We've heard them so many times that we no longer are capable of really hearing them. We think, "Of course God is pleased with Him, duh! He's the Son of God who sacrificed His life for poor wretched sinners."

Let's pause and consider *when* God the Father spoke these words to Jesus. At this point in Jesus's life, He had not begun his public ministry; he had not performed any public miracles; He had not healed lepers, cured the sick, raised the dead, or healed the blind. In fact, He lived a very normal, unnoticed life. Considering this, how could God the Father be pleased with Jesus? What did Jesus do to deserve such praise?

Up to this point, our Lord lived in obscurity, secrecy, and hiddenness, serving His mother and father in Nazareth. Jesus had not accomplished anything spectacular or groundbreaking. Rather, He submitted in obedience to His parents, fulfilling the common duties and responsibilities of a faithful son without notoriety or fanfare. God the Father loved and loves Jesus because Jesus was and is His Son. God loved Jesus for who He was and is, not for anything He did.

Jesus didn't need man's approval because He knew that He was approved of and loved by His father. In fact, St. John is adamant on this point: "But Jesus did not trust himself unto them for that he knew all men and because he needed not that any should give testimony of man; for he knew what was in man" (Jn 2:24–25).

The more that you and I believe that we are loved, chosen, delighted in by God, the less we will pursue the praises of men. The less we pursue the praises of men, the more we can be who God created us to be. The more that we become who

God created us to be, the more we are truly free. At this point we become a Terror of Demons because the devil cannot convince us to bow down to human respect. Human respect is shifting sand upon which no man should build his house. The love of human respect conditions us to change our identity for the purpose of gaining and maintaining public approval and human affirmation. This is social slavery.

This is why vain ambitions "namely, the love of human praise is hostile to godly faith."[26] A true son of God has faith in his heavenly Father. We must believe that the God we cannot see loves us more than the men we can see who pay us tribute.

"Without faith it is impossible to please God" (Heb 11:6). Trust in God and His fatherhood is the key to everything. Trust is born from faith that God doesn't make junk. God made me; therefore I am not junk. When we trust that God created us "through Him, and in Him, and for Him" (see Col 1), and that "He wills to accomplish in us immeasurably more than we ask or imagine, according to his power that is at work within us" (Eph 3:20), we overcome the temptation to be the dog who returns to the vomit of human praise (see Prov 26:11).

Our Lord Jesus' baptism is a window through which we can "see" God the Father's love for us. God affirmed His Son directly after His baptism with the words: "You are My beloved Son, with whom I am well pleased" (Mk 1:11). This indicates that after we are baptized, the Father claims us as His own in Christ. We are His beloved sons and daughters. He loves us not because of anything we have accomplished, but simply because we are His. If only we could receive this good news.

A couple of years ago, I was giving a keynote address at a Catholic men's conference. Prior to my talk a man introduced himself to me. Within seconds I realized that his interest was not in getting to know me, but in me getting to know all about him. As he began explaining who he was, he showed me several self-made flyers that listed his notable accomplishments, including hosting a television series, and lists of his articles and books that had been published.

At this point he digressed, expressing no small amount of disappointment in the producers who had cancelled his television show. He proceeded to share his discontent that he was not one of the keynotes at the conference. He concluded our conversation by disclosing that many Catholic publishers were unfairly boycotting him, not allowing him access to their acquisition editors.

I know the feeling of rejection. The silence after submitting a manuscript to a publisher can be very disheartening. His pain was obvious. But the pain wasn't because his show was cancelled or that he couldn't get published. The pain was because he forgot that he had a Father in heaven who loved him more than he could love himself.

The Lord asks us, "Am I not enough for you? Am I not sufficient?" Without realizing it, our lived response all too often is, "No. You are not enough."

Recently, a publisher rejected one of my manuscripts. No matter how much I insisted that this was God's will, or that the rejection would make me stronger, and that I would "do better next time," I could not convince myself that this rejection was a good thing, because it felt so terrible.

I decided to take a little time off work and spend an hour at the local church with our Lord in the Most Blessed Sacrament. I didn't talk that hour. Neither did God. It was a long, silent hour without a hint of consolation. I returned to work.

No sooner had I sat in my seat behind my computer then a thought crashed upon my disheartened soul:

"Devin, there are only two things that I require of you: to know and believe with your entire being that I love you. The second: regardless of what you are enduring, return that love to me."

I was stunned. I sat motionless. Suddenly I scrambled for a pen and a piece of paper, hastily wrote it down lest I forget the profound insight. After I captured the thought on paper, I wrote beneath those words, "Do this and I will be free." When I do these two things, I am free. When I don't, I become the devil's marionette. When you know that God loves you, you are liberated from the slavery of human approval, accolades, and evaluations.

If we are honest, somewhere deep in the untouchable realm of our soul lives this pure desire to be great, or as the philosophers called it, to be magnanimous. Magnanimity is from the Latin word *magnanimatas*, which is derived from the two Latin word *magna*, big, and *animus*, soul or spirit. In other words, magnanimity is the virtue of being great of mind and of heart.

The magnanimous man refuses to be petty. Human honor is of little account to him. "I do not accept glory from men"

(Jn 5:41) is the definitive spiritual posture of Jesus and of the magnanimous man.

The ancient Greek philosophers tell us that the magnanimous man thinks little of power and wealth. Recall that after our Lord fed the multitudes with the multiplication of the loaves that they were ready to carry Him off as their king, but Jesus fled to the mountains (see Jn 6:15). This is magnanimity.

The opinion of the populace doesn't sway Jesus from His life's mission, nor should it move us from our mission. The magnanimous man cares for God's truth rather than people's opinions; for He knows that public opinion will enslave him, but the truth will set him free (Jn 8:31).

Being of great heart and mind (magnanimity) and the way of secrecy are flip sides of the same coin. The magnanimous man does not feel compelled to boast, to prove his point, or to be petty. He has a deep inner strength that enables him to press on in secret service of the Lord. Ironically, because this secret service, this quiet, resilient strength embodied in the magnanimous man is so different from the men of his culture, his secret becomes visible in the way that light is visible. We cannot see light as we see an object. We see light because it allows us to see the object. The magnanimous man's life allows the goodness of God to become visible to those he encounters.

Pier Giorgio Frassati was such a man. Born in Italy in the year 1901, Pier was the son of Alfredo Frassati, an agnostic who was the founder and director of the popular newspaper *La Stampa*, and Adelaide Ametis, a renowned painter.

At the age of twenty-four, Pier contracted poliomyelitis, a disease that caused lethal paralysis to his muscles and respiratory system. During the last seven years of his life, Pier secretly served the less fortunate, giving them his time, money, and compassion. At his funeral, the streets of Turin were lined with a multitude of mourners, including the poor and unknown who had benefited from Pier's charity.

Ironically, many of Pier Giorgio's mourners were not aware that he was an heir of the influential Frassati family, and his parents were not aware that Pier was an heir of Jesus Christ. Truly, what is hidden, God will reveal. It was the revelation of Pier's secret acts of charity that influenced Alfredo, his father, to return to the sacraments and the Church.

To be *lathra*, secret, is to be confident that regardless of how unknown or unheralded you are, you know that you are known by God. The secret son of God believes that he has the biggest and best audience—his Father in Heaven—and is not concerned with fans and followers. You see, when you believe people's opinion of you, you will never be enough. When you believe in God's love for you, He will always be enough.

Our Lord's first public miracle occurred at a wedding in Cana of Galilee when the newly wedded couple's feast was temporarily hindered when the wine ran out (see Jn 2:1–12). In our Lord's time, a wedding feast lasted seven days, and people traveled for miles to attend. To run out of wine midway through the wedding was socially devastating.

Mary, the Mother of Jesus, discreetely prompts Him to perform a miracle, to help the young couple avoid embarrassment and shame. Our Lord Jesus discreetly commands the servants to fill the jars, used for ceremonial baptismal washings, with water.

The servants obediently filled the jars, each holding twenty to thirty gallons, to the brim. Then Jesus commands the servants to take the water, which had now turned wine, to the chief steward of the feast. "When the chief steward had tasted the water made wine, and knew not where the wine had come from, but the waiters knew who had drawn the water; the chief steward calleth the bridegroom and saith to him: every man [serves] first the good wine; and when men have drunk freely then that which is worse. But thou hast kept the good wine until now" (Jn 2:9–10).

Notice that the chief steward did not know from where the wine came. Our Lord performed his "public" miracle in secret. Yet, this miracle became public knowledge.

Give to God your water, your secret works, and He will transform them into wine, into grace. Like the servants, fill your jars to the brim, do everything with excellence, that is without boasting or complaining. Do it all for the glory of God. For "a man should take care of his good name to provide good things in the sight of God and men, yet without taking empty pleasure in human praise."[27]

Our God desires to share His glory with those who act in faith, with those who believe that God can do more with our secret works than the loud and proud can do with their social media platforms.

Without Jesus, our water—regardless of how many views and hits it has—will never become wine; and Jesus will not make wine without your water, without your secret works. God wants a partnership with us.

Give to God your secret works, your water, and He will transform them into wine, for He cannot and will not be outdone in generosity. This is the secret behind secret power.

CHAPTER 4

Passion's Power

There are many scenes from motion pictures that are forever seared into my memory, but few of them remain as vivid and disturbing as the haunting scene from Steven Spielberg's epic film *Saving Private Ryan*. Forever etched in my mind is the scandalously weak character, Private Upham, one of seven soldiers that Captain Miller selected to fulfill the mission of finding and saving Private Ryan.

The setting is World War II. Upham is an interpreter, and a naïve pacifist who doesn't comprehend the brutality of war, the evil of the enemy, and that people who are inhumane exist. After converging upon a German outpost, they capture a German gunman, whom Upham befriends and convinces Miller to release.

Later the squad attempts to overtake a building occupied by Germans, including the German gunman that Miller set free. Everyone is killed except for the German gunman and Mellish, one of Upham's American comrades. Hand-to-hand combat ensues and a knife is drawn, while Upham sits motionless outside the room where the fight is occurring.

It appeared that Mellish was winning the brawl but becoming exhausted; the German gunman gained the upper hand and pinned Mellish's back to the ground while slowly, relentlessly, pressing a dagger downward toward Mellish's chest. Mellish pleads for the German to have mercy. The German continues to press the knife toward Mellish's chest. The scene is nearly paralyzing in suspense and is difficult to watch. I remember thinking as I watched, "Upham will surely enter, blow the German's head off, and save Mellish." But he didn't.

Emotionally incapacitated, armed with a loaded weapon and with the squad's .30-caliber ammo, bullet belts draped around his neck, Upham sits motionless, tears streaming down his face, as he listens to his comrade plead for his life . . . and yet he does nothing to rescue him.

Mellish's strength finally fails, and the German presses the knife into his chest, killing him.

Afterward, the German exits the scene, walking past the emotionally distraught, harmless Upham, giving him a look of scorn combined with a sinister, demeaning smile.

The night that I watched *Saving Private Ryan* I couldn't sleep. My mind repeatedly returned to that haunting scene. I know it is only a movie. Yet, I found myself enraged at Upham's lack of loyalty, his lack of courage, and his unwillingness to risk his life to defend his own. Why did Upham unsettle me?

Spielberg's portrayal of a fully armed pacifist who does nothing to defend his own is a fitting image of many a modern Christian man. We've been conditioned to believe that the devil and his minions are myths. We conclude that we have no real nemesis. The only enemy is the one who doesn't "get along" with others, who doesn't play Mr. Nice Guy; the only enemy is the man who is disagreeable.

We've been taught at length that Jesus is the ultimate Mr. Nice Guy, confirmed by His own description of Himself as meek and humble of heart. Meek and humble He is. But there is more to our Savior than gentle kindness. Half-truths don't make men whole. Hiding, or refraining from disclosing the entire truth, is the devil's tactic: he makes a lie believable by proposing half of the truth.

Though Jesus was meek and humble of heart, He nevertheless was a relentless, courageous conqueror who never shied away from a necessary conflict when the truth and the salvation of souls were on the line. Our Lord wasn't afraid of taking on a multitude of money changers, overturning their tables and like lightning, with his whip of chords, thrashing and executing judgment on those who were buying and selling in His Father's house. With an unyielding force, he drove out those religious usurpers for the purpose of reclaiming His Father's house as a place of worship. And the very next day, early in the morning, he had the audacity to take up His place in that temple and teach the multitudes. Jesus is fearless.

Jesus was anything but a really nice guy. Nevertheless the modern Christian man has been conditioned to believe that to follow Christ is to be nothing more than a nice guy who avoids conflict at all cost. His only identifiable enemy is being confrontational or disagreeable. Conflict is the great evil that the nice guy must overcome no matter what. It is little wonder why men have left the Church in droves. Men have very little interest in being a Christian Mr. Rogers.

If I were explaining these ideas to one of these nice guys, he would respond by smiling consistently, repeatedly nodding his head to signal that he was tracking with me (whether he agreed or not). And if his belief ran contrary to my proposals, I would never know it because he would be too fearful to admit it. The nice guy is plagued by an undermining devilish fear: the loss of being liked and included. After all, isn't that what church community is all about—inclusion? A lot of us will be shocked at how non-inclusive God will be on Judgment Day.

Our nice guy is unwilling to die on any mountain of truth, because in his mind there are no mountains worthy of climbing, nor any cross or any truth worthy of carrying up that lonely mountain, nor any death worth dying.

The Greeks believed in and honored manliness, *andreia*.[28] Essential to *andreia* was *thymos*. *Thymos* was such an important and vital part of manliness and the journey toward ultimate *andreia* that it is mentioned over seven hundred times in Homer's *Iliad* and *Odyssey*.[29] Plato believed that thymos was a rational kind of courage that enabled a man to conquer fear in spite of pleasure or pain in the fight for that which is just and good.[30]

St. Thomas Aquinas defines thymos more precisely as a power in the irascible (spirited) passions. When faced with overcoming evil for the purpose of achieving a good, thymos is the power that is activated within us. Again, "Thymos is the irascible passion that overcomes obstacles."[31]

Thymos is awakened and engaged and highly necessary in difficult and arduous matters. St. Thomas tells us that anger is caused by a difficult evil already present. When this evil presents itself, a person has two choices: to succumb to it, or to launch an attack on the hurtful evil, which is a movement of righteous spiritedness that can be characterized by anger.[32] In other words, when faced with evil, you will either become angry and attack the evil, or fall to the temptation presented.

Our passions are naturally directed toward what is good, or to reject what is evil. This is how God made us. The pure soul is saddened by murder, rape, poverty, and genocide. The pure soul is not attracted to people being bullied or dominated. A pure soul is attracted to love, beauty, and order. This is why so many people get married and have families: they are attracted to the goodness of relational love.

St. Thomas segments the passions into two categories. The first are the concupiscible (desirous) passions, which he pairs in twos: love and hate; desire and aversion; joy and sadness. These passions are awakened at two stages: the desire, and the repose (rest) that comes after attaining it.

But often there is a middle stage between desire and repose, which involves moving toward a good by facing and overcoming an evil. This stage St. Thomas identifies as the irascible (spirited) passions, which he also lists in pairs: hope and despair; fear and daring; and anger. Now anger has no opposite passion other than surrender or passivity. Being passive is not a passion. It is an absence of passion, much like sin is an absence of good. In other words, something good is missing.

So sometimes we are compelled to face a perceived bad or evil for the intent of obtaining a good; or we are compelled to deprive ourselves of a perceived good to obtain a greater good. This is where the irascible, spirited passions kick in.

The irascible sense responds to a greater good that is at stake by compulsively making a sacrifice. For example, a child

is crossing the street into oncoming traffic. Thymos, the irascible passions, compel you to place yourself between the car
and the child. An elderly man is being mobbed, and suddenly
your anger flares and you jump into the scene to spare him.

"Thymos is more clearly associated with anger. It is a special kind of anger activated when a man's honor is violated,
when his reputation is on the line, when his family and prop-
erty are threatened. It drives a man to stand up for his country, his loved one."[33]

In effect, thymos is closely related to righteous indignation,
a justified anger that compels a person to do battle for what
is just, right, and honorable. That hatred of evil and sin is the
irascible power. Upham lacked thymos; Jesus had it in spades.

The passion of anger, in its positive form, if channeled by
thymos can empower a man to overcome fear and conquer
great evil in order to obtain a noble goal.

So why is this important? Ask yourself: When was the last
time I heard about thymos, or the necessity of it? When was
the last time someone spoke of righteous anger and explained
how to channel it? When was the last time you heard anyone
talk about manliness, courage, and what it takes to embody

both? The reason this is so important is precisely because very few people think it is important. In other words, when people forget something important, they fall into great error. The exercise of thymos has become a lost art. Our culture has conditioned us to believe that anger is completely evil, and that the greatest virtue is "getting along" with everyone. But to get along with everyone, you will not challenge anyone, nor will anyone challenge you, and when no one is challenged, no one grows, and when people don't grow, their souls die.

Those who propagate the virtue of "getting along" package it in a powerful word called "peace." It has become the centerpiece of slogans and church hymns: Peace on earth. Peace in the Middle East. Let there be peace on earth and let it begin with me.

This kind of peace has absolutely nothing to do with Christianity, whose Founder said, "I did not come to bring peace, but a sword" (see Mt 10:34). To believe that there is only one way, one truth, and one life; and that this way, truth, and life is the person Jesus Christ who sacrificed Himself to conquer the devil, to deliver man from the shackles of sin, to ransom humanity from eternal damnation, is to be an obstacle to the world's version of "peace," and is to be in constant conflict with the devil. Because those who propagate the virtue of getting along avoid Truth at all cost. Because truth challenges. Truth brings the sword. Truth exposes our error, our sin, and very few people relish that type of conviction.

The world's peace discriminates against the truth and vilifies those who profess it as the bullies, the unsympathetic rigorists, the haters of human progressivism.

The Upham brand of pacifism and Christ's Sword are incompatible. The world is full of Uphams who are afraid of rocking the boat and therefore become proponents of the world's peace. The man who builds his life upon the world's ideal of peace is a spiritual pacifist who is unwilling to stake his life on the fact that there is only one Savior, one Truth, one God, and that there is only one Way to Him.

Though wrath may be one of the seven deadly sins, nevertheless righteous anger is virtuous and is channeled by thymos. It is important that we not only believe this truth but learn how to apply it to our lives. When we encounter tremendous challenges, when we are mandated to battle for good and truth, when we must stand our ground and maintain and proclaim our moral beliefs in the face of great persecution, thymos is needed. Thymos is the power to embrace the challenge, face the fear, and sacrifice and suffer to overcome great evil.

We may not realize it, but thymos is necessary in the most common aspects of our life. When you battle to rise early in the morning for prayer you are sacrificing the perceived good of sleep, fighting sloth and the devil for the greater good of communion with God; when you abstain from sweets during Lent you are sacrificing the perceived good of tasteful pleasure for the greater good of participating with God in the salvation of souls; when you fight for your marriage by embracing the perceived bad of the discomfort of discussing your problems for the greater good of a deeper harmony, vulnerability, and real peace—that is thymos.

Thymos is what enables a man to rise to the challenge in the most difficult situations to achieve a noble good.

A powerful example that demonstrates the relationship between thymos and anger is the account of St. Thomas Aquinas's temptation. St. Thomas was the youngest son of very wealthy parents who expected him to join the prestigious Benedictine monastery. Thomas had other plans. To his parent's dismay, Thomas had decided to become a Dominican, which meant that he would take a vow of poverty and become a beggar. His family was ashamed of his decision. So to dissuade him from becoming a Dominican his family kidnapped him and imprisoned him in the family castle until he would retract his decision.

At one point, his brothers hired a prostitute to seduce Thomas so that he would abandon his vow of chastity. The scantily clad woman arrived at Thomas's room. Thomas responded by yelling and grabbing a log from the fireplace, chasing her out of the room, slamming the door behind her, then making the sign of the cross with the ashes from the log.

Thomas demonstrated thymos in action, which activated the passion of righteous anger, empowering him to overcome the evil and apprehend the good of chastity. If Thomas had been a nice guy, for fear of offending her he would have had the young lady sit down for tea, and before long, Thomas could have been seduced. And that nice guy would not have become the greatest doctor in Catholic Church history. Thomas was a fighter through and through. How else could someone write the massive volumes of the Summa Theologica, which not only defined our faith, but also combated heresy?

The nice guy syndrome has not only affected the way we envision Jesus, but also the way we view His virginal father, St. Joseph. St. Joseph is often depicted as a harmless, benign, elderly creature, lacking signs of any virility.

In depictions of the Holy Family, Joseph is often to the side, his balding head lurking in the shadows, his tired, aged body leaning on a staff, while he holds a beautiful bouquet of flowers. To anyone who didn't grow up Catholic, they may think that the ol' man in the stained-glass window of the nativity scene is Mary's grandpa.

I know, I know. I understand that the lily richly represents St. Joseph's purity and chastity. But have you ever attempted to envision St. Joseph trying to plow a field, frame the walls of his house, thatch a roof, or pound a nail with one of those delicate little lilies?

I think we are afraid of making St. Joseph appear too masculine, too young, too virile because we associate those things with the age of unbridled lust. We cannot imagine someone so strong, young, and masculine being so pure and chaste. To ease the mental challenge we give St. Joseph the appearance of one who literally could not lust—even if he tried.

This typification of the soft St. Joseph has also seeped into other areas of his life. For example, my fourteen-year-old daughter and her friends were playing charades. Each person had to pretend to be a saint, and the others would guess which saint it was. (I know, we homeschool). One of her friends laid down and acted as though she was sleeping. To which someone blurted out, "St. Joseph!"

Was St. Joseph a soft, sleepy, delicate, harmless, elderly man who lacked virility, strength and thymos? Judging by the depiction in many of our churches you would think so. But let's examine this.

St. Matthew's Gospel recounts that after Joseph discovered Mary pregnant and was deciding to put her away privately, "while he thought on these things, an angel of the Lord appeared to him in his sleep" (Mt 1:20). Initially, it appears that St. Joseph is sleeping on the job. But the Greek word used for "while he thought" or "as he pondered" is *enthymeomai* (from *en*, meaning in a state or condition, and intensifying *thymos*, meaning a passionate response), signifying a passionate frame of mind, or being quickly moved by strong, provoking impulses.[34]

This indicates that St. Joseph's act of pondering over his personal dilemma was not mere casual consideration, but rather an intense, spirit-rending event. St. Joseph wrestled with himself over the situation. On one hand he loved his wife, Mary, and desired to be her faithful husband. Yet, on the other hand, he was resolute in doing God's will, even at the cost of his desires.

Joseph's soul was deeply grieved by the potential loss of Mary, but he refused to surrender the battle. He pressed on, seeking God's face, and was determined to ponder the situation, hoping for a divine resolution.

Recall that St. Thomas indicates that thymos, the root word of *enthymeomai*, is the part of the soul that combats those things that attempt to attack a precious good. Much like Jesus driving out the buyers and sellers from the temple and St. Thomas overcoming the prostitute's seduction, St. Joseph combated the devil over the precious good of Mary and his marriage to her. He was tormented by the idea of separating himself from her, and therefore he would not give up on her or on God.

St. Joseph is anything but a passive nice guy who went home to make flower arrangements. Rather he entered the ring, pressed the matter, stood his ground, and waited on God in an effort to obtain the good.

This battle was so arduous and intense that Joseph, worn from the dilemma, finally falls asleep, and it is then that his sleep is interrupted with the apparition of the angel commanding him to take Mary into his home. Thymos played a vital role in helping Joseph passionately pursue what is right. Joseph was willing to surrender the perceived good of Mary being his wife, an action which appeared to be bad for him, in exchange for doing God's will. That's thymos. Additionally, Joseph eventually embraced the perceived bad of a lifetime of marital celibacy for the greater good of honoring and protecting the Holy Virgin's profound, intimate communion with God. That's a real man; that's thymos.

But notice what Joseph did not do. He didn't vent his anger on Mary. He didn't complain against God. He didn't bang out nasty tweets: #mylifestinks #mywifeispregnantandImnotthe-father.

No. In secret, in the silence, he remained steady in faith, doing four simple things: first, he took his desire, his hope, his fears, all of his passions, and **entered the silence**. Second, he submitted his passion in prayer to God. Joseph's thymos kicked in, giving him the power to fight against despair, hopelessness, and futility. *He prayed passionately.* Third, he waited on God. We don't know if Joseph waited three hours, three days, three weeks, or three months. Regardless, he **waited in faith** and did not give up on God. Fourth, he **repeated those three steps** again and again until God directed him. Joseph was a fighter.

Thymos isn't only about fighting outside enemies. Plato said that ultimately the purpose of thymos is to conquer ourselves, to govern our evil inclinations and passions. Sometimes the bigger fight is to overcome rash reactions. Social media platforms afford us the unique capability of firing away and blasting those we don't agree with instantaneously. Soon after, regret sets in. Our lack of mastery over our thymos is destroying relationships and dividing the Church. And yet, this is no excuse to not engage it and learn to use it properly. You don't stop eating because you haven't learned how to control your appetite. Rather, you train yourself.

St. Joseph teaches us that the biggest fight is nearly always against ourselves in the attempt to channel our passions for good.

Whether you are suddenly awakened and called upon by God to deprive yourself of the good of sleep to pray at the 3:00 a.m. hour for the salvation of souls; or are faced with the compelling need to deprive yourself of the good of marital intercourse for the purpose of your spouse's sanity; or are driven to write a letter of fraternal correction to a bishop who has become a hireling; be not afraid of using your thymos.

We often toggle between repression and indulgence. We extinguish our thymos for fear that we can do serious damage in our fight for good. Remember Upham? He was fully armed, yet afraid to use that power. Or we take the Rambo, take-no-prisoners approach, needlessly damaging relationships. Virtue is power in the middle. We must not repress our thymos nor let it run unbridled. Thymos properly channeled is passion's power that enables you to be like St. Joseph, overcome obstacles, vanquish vice, conquer evil, and be a terror of demons.

CHAPTER 5

Obedience's Power

Imagine for a moment a world lacking order. For example, the typical thirty minutes spent shopping at the grocery store will now demand the lion's share of your day to locate what you are looking for. Why? Because the grocery store is no longer tightly organized and categorically segmented. Instead of an orderly grocery store it resembles an antique store. Food is everywhere. Piles upon piles of foods from different departments are mixed together.

Some boxes of cereal—but not all—are peppered among some of the produce. Varying types of vegetables and fruits are mixed together in large baskets or strewn randomly amidst the candy. Deli meats, at least some of them, are mixed in with some of the dairy products; meat products are also sprinkled among toiletry items; diapers are located in the delicatessen—but not all of them. The experience is like a grown-up Easter egg hunt; people digging frantically through shelf after shelf, basket after basket, hoping to find where the Twizzlers are hiding. To make matters worse, no one knows where the coffee is; and the stock boy is out for a smoke.

Fast food drive-throughs are handled on a first-come first-served basis. You may have ordered first, but if the car behind you arrives at the delivery window before you, he gets your order. Cars step out of line, jockeying for space. The experience is like driving amidst a sea of taxi drivers in downtown New York City.

Orders are displaced. But that isn't the worst of it. Ingredients are also displaced. Pickles and ketchup are sometimes placed on top of the bun—if they remembered to use a bun. On other occasions, your slice of cheese is not on the bottom bun, but on the bottom of the bottom bun. This situation becomes a bit sticky (literally) if they forgot to wrap your sandwich—which happens occasionally.

The education "system" has randomly decided that your kindergarten daughter, who hasn't learned addition, will be taught advanced algebra in a classroom that has a combination of beanbag chairs, La-Z-Boy recliners, and blow-up mattresses.

Employees arrive at the workplace whenever they feel like it and for as long or as short a period of time as they feel is necessary.

The government mandates that during the spring months days will be nights, and during the fall months, nights will be days (and we thought Daylight Saving Time was difficult to deal with).

Families don't have any hierarchical order. Each family member, regardless of age or experience, can choose whether they want to be a parent, a child, or the household pet.

The military ceases to have captains and corporals, sergeants, and strategies. It is simply guys and gals with guns.

People are supposed to pay for their purchases, but if you can steal and get away with it, all the power to you. If you are a store owner, don't bother calling the police patrol. Their hours are random, and so is the cell phone service in your area.

Traffic and tax laws are consistently disregarded. The economy tanks and traffic accidents go through the roof.

When order is lacking, chaos ensues. Human beings cannot withstand prolonged periods of unpredictability, confusion, and anarchy. We crave and actually need a well-ordered life, a well-ordered society.

But let's take this imaginary exercise a little further—or actually a little *closer* to our current reality.

A man places a jar of peanut butter on the cashier's conveyer belt. The cashier, who is biologically male, but believes that he is a female, rings the peanut butter up and says, "That will be $4.39."

The man responds, "I'm sorry sir. You are mistaken . . . it should ring up at ninety-nine cents."

The cashier looks at him as though he is crazy. "First, please don't call me sir—I'm a woman. Second, there is no current sale on the peanut butter."

Disgruntled, our shopper responds with a sharper tone, "Who said anything about peanut butter—that's a bunch of bananas, and bananas are on sale for ninety-nine cents."

"Sir, you're wrong," our cashier snaps back. "It's a jar of

peanut butter . . . anyone in their right mind can tell that it's a jar of peanut butter. Maybe you're the one who is bananas."

A very athletically talented, middle-school, biologically male basketball player wakes up one morning with the revelation that he is actually a girl. The school allows him to join the girls' basketball team, and consequently he dominates the conference in scoring.

As our superstar leaves the gymnasium, with his purse dangling from his broad shoulder, a tag team of less-fortunate gypsies assaults him, one bumping him to distract him, while the other steals his purse, containing his credit cards and cash.

"Stop! Thief! They stole my purse!"

A priest lives next door to an atheist homosexual couple. He asks if he can use their home as the setting for his Christmas Day Mass. The couple politely refuses. "We really don't believe in all that Catholic stuff." The priest files a lawsuit for discrimination against the couple and wins . . . But how can that be? Isn't there such a thing as separation between church and state?

Do you see the logical, or illogical, thread? Order is based on truth. When truth is lacking, anyone can make up their own truth. Now that might be acceptable if the person making the truth didn't demand others to acknowledge their lie as the truth. In other words, those who make up their own truth want to impose that "truth" on others, demanding that others lie and deny the actual truth for the purpose of upholding their fabricated version of truth.

A transgender person cannot mandate that another person refer to him or her by a sex that is not his or her biological sex any more than a person can mandate that a cashier believe that peanut butter is a bunch of bananas just because a customer says it is.

People should not permit boys who feel like girls to rob girls of the fun they derive from playing sports. Nor should boys who feel like girls be permitted to steal a future, and a potential scholarship, from girls who play sports, any more than a person can say it is morally acceptable to steal someone's wallet and hard-earned cash, just because the robber claims that he has a "right" to level the wealth status among human beings.

Same-sex couples cannot demand that their beliefs and marriages be recognized by and celebrated in the Catholic

Church any more than a priest has a right to that same-sex couple's home for his Christmas Day Mass. There is a separation between church and state. And that separation means that the two remain separate. Just because the government legally permits same-sex marriages, that approval has no bearing on the Church and her theology.

Progressives can pretend that a lie is the truth, but demanding that another person has to proclaim their lie at the expense of the truth is a double standard.

When this occurs, a person's lie becomes a dictating tyrant that negates another person's ability to profess the truth. Freedom of speech does not mean that people who believe a lie can suppress and silence those who know and believe the truth.

I realize that to use the word *lie* is very offensive to a person who believes or feels that the lie is the truth about themselves. The definition of the verb *lie* is to make an untrue or inaccurate statement with the intent to deceive, or to create a false or misleading impression. A lie is something that misleads or deceives. This is not my definition, but this is an accurate description of an action that denies fundamental truths such as biological sex.

'Trans-truth" is a lie because it denies transcendent truth. Truth doesn't change, regardless of how much a person says that it has changed. If truth doesn't change, then "sex change" cannot be true . . . it is a lie, because biological sex doesn't actually change. That is the truth. Regardless how well the sex change operation goes, a man who becomes a woman cannot become pregnant. A woman who becomes a man cannot impregnate a woman. The only change is superficial.

Ultimately people who want to dismiss the truth do so by saying that it doesn't exist. When a person says that there is no truth, they believe that what they are professing is *the* truth, and that you better believe it.

But what they actually mean to say is that they will not accept Truth; and therefore they will fabricate their own. Defining your own "trans-truth" is "wis-dumb." Living by God's transcendent truth is wisdom.

This is very long-winded way of demonstrating the logical, or actually the illogical, trajectory of a world without order.

Whether it is the consistency of the sunrise and sunset; the earth remaining fixed in space as it rotates on its axis at 23.5 degrees; the paths of the planets of the solar system never intersecting; the majority of human beings not murdering their neighbors; or boys pretending to be cowboys and girls wanting to be mommies, there is an inescapable order to all of existence.

Yet, this is precisely what the post-Christian culture is attempting to undermine. It attempts to escape order by trying to avoid the truth. But why? Because if there is no order, then there is no hierarchy of power; and if there is no hierarchy of power, then there is no authority; if there is no authority, there are no laws; and if there are no laws, there are no commands; and if there are no commands, no obedience is demanded; and if no obedience is demanded, there are no limits imposed on any individual. This is perceived as unlimited personal power.

But there is a hierarchy of power: God all-powerful is at the top of this chain of command. The second tier consists of human beings who are subject to God; and lastly, creatures that are subject to man, angels, and ultimately God.

God is the ultimate authority; He shares His authority with the angels and with man by means of laws and commands, and it is to these commands that we must obediently submit. By submitting to God's commands, we are professing by our actions that God is God, and we are not. This is important. The very first temptation that the devil proposed to human beings was "to be like God knowing good and evil" (Gen 3:5). In other words, the devil promised our first parents that they could determine truth—what is good and what is evil—for themselves. They did not need God to help them with that; and since they did not need God's guidance regarding matters of moral judgments, they could in effect be their own gods. The more things change, the more things stay the same. History does repeat itself—and so does human beings' tendency to sin.

Now, there are two types of people who disobey God's order of creation: those who believe they can lie and say that their lie is the truth; and those who are intelligent enough to realize that they cannot make a lie true, and so dismiss God altogether by saying that He does not exist.

Our current culture has people in both camps. I believe that the devil enjoys using the people in the first camp, who are foolish enough to say that a lie is truth, to demonstrate to God how stupid human beings can be. It is not enough that the devil incites men to rebel against God while they know that God exists. He wants to rub humanity's nose in the poop of absurdity by enticing them to believe that they can change truth.

Not only does a hierarchical order exist in creation, but it also exists within the human creature himself. God created man to be properly ordered in himself, and by means of this order, man could be free to love without being enslaved and vexed by selfishness.

God gave man an intellect that is to be primary in his personal hierarchical order. The intellect determines right from wrong, good from evil. The will acts upon and follows the intellect's decision to do right, to pursue the good. The will then subdues, channels, and engages the power of the passions to fuel the person to follow through with the accomplishment of a noble and good action. After our first parent's original sin, that original order became compromised and disordered.

Suddenly their personal order became disordered, and the hierarchical order of the intellect, will, and passions became inverted; and from this point on the passions fight to drive the will, and the will attempts to subdue the intellect. This is truly a grave injustice, because this disorder within the human being tortures us, as attested by St. Paul: "The things that I don't want to do, I do; and the very thing I want to do, I don't do . . ." (see Rom 7:15).

When the order of the human being becomes inverted, disorder runs rampant, selfishness rules, and depression, anxiety, loneliness, and hopelessness become the normal human condition.

When we fail at maintaining a proper order within ourselves, our marriages end in divorce, our families are separated, and soon society becomes disjointed and impoverished on many levels. Before you know it, peanut butter is bananas, boys are girls, stealing is equality, and the state is the church, and the church succumbs to the state.

What's the point of all of this? Obedience is the key to order, the key to conquering self. As Pope St. Gregory the Great says, "When we humbly give way to another's voice, we overcome ourselves in our hearts."[35] Obedience is the key to detachment from selfishness. Obedience is the key to protecting and instilling all of the virtues. Again, to quote Gregory the Great, "Obedience is the only virtue that ingrafts [and protects (Aquinas)] the virtues in the soul."[36] This indicates that obedience is the key to having real power. Remember, power is virtue, which means that obedience is the secret means to being truly powerful.

It is little wonder that the Promoter of the Faith—an office of the Catholic Church that acted as the *advocatus diaboli*, devil's advocate—had the duty of critically examining the life of an individual proposed for beatification by first examining whether that individual was obedient to his or her superiors.

This brings to mind the heroic example of St. Padre Pio. Padre Pio was an Italian friar, priest, mystic, and stigmatist—that is, one who bore the wounds of Christ's Passion and Crucifixion in his body. People from all over the world flocked to San Giovanni Rotondo, Italy, hoping to witness him offer the Holy Sacrifice of the Mass, confess their sins to him, or simply see him from afar.

As his fame spread, jealousy of him within the hierarchy of the Church intensified. From 1921 to 1922 officials at the Vatican imposed severe restrictions on Padre Pio, forbidding him to offer the Holy Sacrifice of the Mass in public or to hear confessions. No longer was he allowed to bless people, respond to letters, or show his stigmata publicly. The Holy See made several statements up until 1931 that the mystical occurrences in Padre Pio's life had no divine cause. Padre Pio responded to his superior's orders with total submission and humble obedience.

Finally, in 1934 Pope Pius XI ordered a reversal of the sanctions imposed upon Padre Pio, and in the mid 1960s Pope Paul VI dismissed all allegations against him.

The obedient man, like Padre Pio, may appear, initially, to be weak, because his will is subject to a superior who exercises authority over him. However, obedience is actually a demonstration of a deep, mature, interior strength; an unwavering trust that God sees our actions and rewards our fidelity.

There are three hallmarks or components to true obedience. First, acknowledgment of and submission to the chain of command. To be obedient, we must know and accept our place in the hierarchical order—who our superiors are. Second, true obedience presupposes that one listens to his commander and receives the command. Third, true obedience is exemplified by using one's will to carry out the command *promptly*. St. Thomas Aquinas tells us that when obedience is prompt, it becomes a special virtue and increases virtue in the individual's soul—particularly when the command is disagreeable to us.

Enter St. Joseph. St. Joseph was consistently and promptly obedient. According to the Scripture, he never wavered in carrying out a command with alacrity.

St. Matthew tells us that after Joseph's annunciation, when the angel told him to take Mary, his wife, into his home, Joseph

[rose] up from sleep, did as the angel of the Lord commanded him and took unto him his wife" (Mt 1:24).

St. Joseph subjected himself to the established and divinely appointed hierarchal order. He reverenced and respected God's divine authority as embodied by the angel of the Lord; and he heeded the angel's commands promptly.

Joseph's prompt obedience was not a single occurrence, but rather was characteristic of his way of life. Joseph was a doer. Whether he fulfilled the commands and precepts of the Law to have Jesus circumcised on the eight day (see Lk 2:21), or have Jesus consecrated to God after the period of Mary's purification had been completed (see Lk 2:22–23) or brought the twelve-year-old Jesus to the temple in Jerusalem to participate in the Feast of the Passover (see Lk 2:41–52), Joseph was obedient to the Torah. Joseph was obedient to secular authorities, such as Caesar who demanded that every Jew be numbered among his census, which meant that Joseph trek with his very pregnant wife from Nazareth to Bethlehem (see Lk 2:3). Joseph was promptly obedient to the Lord by fulfilling the angel's commands to flee to Egypt for the purpose of evading Herod and his soldiers, who launched an attempt to murder the Christ Child (see Mt 2:13), and the command to depart from Egypt and return to Israel after the Christ Child's persecutors had died (see Mt 2:20). Regardless of whether the authority was God, an angel, the Law, or an emperor, Joseph fulfilled the commands of his superiors with prompt obedience, which testifies to his tremendous virtue.

God could depend on St. Joseph to obey his commands, and because of this God entrusted St. Joseph with more responsibility. In fact, God not only entrusted St. Joseph with the Holy Family, but even today He has entrusted the care of the entire Catholic Church to his holy patronage.[37]

What is St. Joseph's secret to being consistently and promptly obedient? The secret is found in the word *obedience* itself. "To obey (from the Latin *ob-audire*, to hear or listen to) in faith is to submit freely to the word that has been *heard*, because its truth is guaranteed by God" (CCC 144, emphasis added).

In other words, an act of obedience begins with the intentional act of listening, particularly to God, His Word, His commands, the superiors whose rule He has placed us under. So obedience and listening are two sides of the same coin—you cannot have one without the other, any more than you can have heads without tails.

There are vast amounts of people who neglect to pray and therefore cannot help but to disobey God. But there also exist those "good Catholics" who pray but don't obey the commands of their superiors, or the demands and responsibilities of their vocational state of life, particularly in the seemingly trivial or insignificant duties.

Often people will go to great lengths to offer to God all sorts of valiant sacrifices in the form of long fasts, harsh punishments to the body, extreme evangelization efforts. But God never asked for any of these things.

"Sacrifice and oblations Thou didst not desire; but an open ear" (Ps 40:7). When we refuse to apply ourselves to the task of listening to God, we often carry out sacrifices that we believe are pleasing to Him, but actually don't please Him in the least.

A prime example of this is King Saul, the first king of Israel, who was commanded by Samuel the prophet of the Lord (who was commanded by God—notice the hierarchy of authority) to utterly destroy the Amalekites and their wickedness.

Saul was commanded to "Go and smite [the Amalekites] and utterly destroy all [they] hath; spare [them] not, nor covet anything that is [theirs], but slay both man and woman, child and suckling, ox and sheep, camel and ass" (1 Sam 15:3).

Now, without hopping down a rabbit hole of human genocide and discussing why God commanded the slaughter of the Amalekites, let's focus on the principle of obedience.

How did Saul respond to the command? He commanded two hundred thousand foot soldiers to carry out this command. (So far so good.) Saul and the Israelites crushed and smote the Amalekites . . . but "Saul spared Agag [the Amalekite king], but all the common people he slew with the edge of the sword; and the best of the flocks of sheep and of the herds, and the garments and the rams, and all that was beautiful, he would not destroy them; but everything that was vile and good for nothing, that they destroyed" (1 Samuel 15:9).

When Samuel the prophet met Saul after his victory, King Saul greeted the prophet, "I have fulfilled the word of the Lord" (1 Samuel 15:13).

An intense dialogue between Samuel and Saul commenced. Saul made the poor excuse that he kept the Amalekites livestock for the purpose of offering sacrifice to God. Samuel rebuked Saul, "Doth the Lord desire holocausts and victims, and not rather that the voice of the Lord should be obeyed? For obedience is better than sacrifices" (1 Samuel 15:22).

"Because [disobedience] is the sin of witchcraft, to rebel like the crime of idolatry, to refuse to obey. For as much therefore as thou hast rejected the word of the Lord, the Lord hath also rejected thee from being king" (1 Samuel 15:22–23).

Did you catch that? To disobey God is devil worship. Why? Because the disobedient man disregards God and His commands in exchange for the devil's promise of living a life without limits. Yet, by embracing the promise of a life without limits, man becomes most limited, because he has severed himself from the unlimited God who can do in him far more than he could hope for or imagine (see Eph 3:20).

"The marked difference between the common man and the saint is that the saint discerns what his master desires by entering the silence and waiting on his divine direction. By waiting in silence on God, he learns to be obedient to His Lord in all things—even those that appear insignificant. The saint learns that obedience is better than sacrifice because obedience is the sacrifice of pride."[38] Or as St. Gregory the Great says, "Obedience is rightly preferred to sacrifices, because by sacrifices, another's body is slain, whereas by obedience we slay our own will."[39]

This "slaying" of our own will purifies us of petty attachments; of the pride of desiring to make "big," "noticed" sacrifices; it purifies us of our selfish motivations; but most of all, it makes us available to God, so that His divine power may work in and through us in extraordinary ways.

Obedience inculcates virtue, and protecting us from pride, it protects the virtues already in us. Virtue, God's power, is increased in us and protected in us, and thus we become powerful in God.

This is why the obedient man, like St. Joseph, is a nuisance and terror to the devil. The demons fear the obedient man because they cannot deter him from fulfilling the Lord's command. God can rely on such a man. The only way the devil can stop the obedient man is to have him assassinated. His only "hope" is that the saint will, under the duress of torture, betray His Lord.

Unfortunately, many of us toggle between being like Saul and St. Joseph. Let's face it, often we are unreliable. If you are reading this book, most likely you have a desire to be on

God's A team. You want to be a starter, on the front lines, and play for our Lord. But have you ever wondered why instead of being on the A team you ride the bench?

Imagine you had a car that started one day, but the next day it didn't. Then it started on each of the following two days. But the following day, it neglected to start. Would you rely on that car? No. You'd junk it. But what if that car is you, and you, in the analogy, are God?

God has a special duty, a command, a mission for you to fulfill; or perhaps it is a seemingly trivial task. One day you show up for prayer, receive the command, and act promptly. The next day you pray, listen, but don't like the command, and thus don't carry it out. The day after, you don't pray at all. You are afraid of what the Lord might command you to do. You eventually feel guilty. But you don't pray. Rather you decide to offer him some sacrifice that you think might impress Him. The next couple of days you forget to pray and neglect to obey.

Do you think that God will entrust you with greater responsibilities? We all want to be on God's A team, but most of us avoid the training sessions and early morning workouts; and that is why we ride the bench.

Many of us are like a quarterback who refuses to run his offensive coach's plays. Thinking that he knows better, the quarterback runs his own plays. The quarterback wants the unlimited freedom to play the game the way he wants. Though our quarterback may get lucky and score a couple of touchdowns, his pattern of self-reliance will lead him and his team to big losses. Pride comes before the fall (see Prov 16:18).

God, the divine coach, knows the devil's strategy. He knows the evil one's strategy inside and out. God knows the field and also knows how to win the game. He simply wants you to listen (in prayer) to Him and to run His plays promptly . . . and be victorious over evil.

There are many people who say that they "know" and "love" God, but rarely listen to what He and His Church tell them about marriage, about contraception, about tithing, about receiving the Most Holy Eucharist when in a marriage not approved by the Church, or about whether Vatican II is a valid council. We simply think that we know better. "But who hath known the mind of the Lord? Or who hath been his counsellor?" (Rom 11:24). "For who hath known the mind of the Lord, that we may instruct Him?" (1 Cor 2:16).

We say things like, "God understands. God loves me. God wants me to be happy. This isn't a big deal to God." Yes, yes, yes, and yes. That is true, but a half-truth. God does understand you. God does love you. God does will your happiness. God does have infinitely broad shoulders that bear the burden of our decisions; and it was those shoulders that carried our decisions, in the form of a heavy wooden cross, up a mountain to where He sacrificed His life.

But there is another half of the truth. God gives us commands that we may learn to be obedient, and by learning to be obedient we conquer ourselves, our pride, our selfishness, and become truly powerful, truly happy.

John the Evangelist sternly warns us, "He who says that he knows God and does not keep His commandments, is a liar . . . but he that keeps His word in him, the charity of God is perfected" (1 Jn 2:4–5). In other words, if you really loved God, you will obey him because obedience is the proof of love.

When anyone considers seriously the idea of obedience, inevitably a thought like this, or something similar arises: "Well that's all great, but am I supposed to obey my superiors, such as my employer, or my parish priest, or secular authorities in all things? What if my employer is immoral, my priest tells me to do something contrary to our Catholic faith, what if the government mandates laws that oppose my religious convictions?"

This is a very important question. Are there limits to obedience? Can I be disobedient? And if so, under what circumstances?

We all have three different types of superiors: God; those who represent God such as a pope, bishop, parish priest, spiritual director; and secular authorities. To these types of superiors we should also add "states" as a kind of "superiors": the *vocational* state and the *present* state, also known as God's will in the present moment.

Regarding God, we are always to obey Him, and in all things (Ex 24:7), without exception. God has communicated His commands with certitude through the authority of the Church, also known as the magisterium, whose teachings align and are supported by both Sacred Tradition and Sacred Scripture. The harmonious integration of these three things provides us with certitude in the discernment of God's commands. The Catholic Church has also provided the faithful with the *Catechism of the Catholic Church* to help us know and understand God's commands clearly.

It is important that we understand and believe this because contemporary theologians have crafted a convincing formula that God's commands, as taught by the Church, are true in a "general sense." However, as the circumstances become more particular and subjective, there may exist "pastoral" reasons why a person should disobey God and His commands.

The first time I encountered this, a "theologian" used the example of a mother who taught Catechism to the youth group at her parish. The next lesson concerned the Church's teaching that homosexual acts are depraved, and same-sex unions are disordered and not blessed by the Church. Yet, her son identified himself as homosexual. This woman and her husband were disheartened and concerned about their son, because he was consistently depressed, lonely, and had very few friends. But wouldn't you know it, the week prior to the Catechism class, their son had his new boyfriend over for dinner. Their son was never happier. This brought tremendous joy to both the mother and the father. Later that night after their son left with his boyfriend, the parents cried with joy because their son was happy and in love.

The theologian asked us, "If you were the mom, what would you do? Would you proceed with teaching the youth at your parish that sexual acts and attraction between homosexuals are disordered as taught by the Church; or would you refrain from sharing this teaching after personally witnessing and subjectively experiencing the joy and love that homosexuals can experience in an intimate, same-sex relationship? Talk about stacking the deck.

After gathering our responses, he said that in a general, objective, more universal sense, the Catechism is correct. But when it comes to personal, subjective circumstances, there could exist factors that negate the Church's teaching, issuing an allowance, such as this young man's newfound happiness stemming from a homosexual relationship.

It is this type of "pastoral" teaching that has severely damaged many people's lives, not to mention endangered their eternal souls.

For example, I was leading a men's retreat centered around John Paul II's Theology of the Body. After the last of the four talks, we had a question-and-answer session. During the Q & A, a man recounted how he and his wife were struggling emotionally and financially after they had their first child. They were afraid of having any more children for fear that the stress would be the final straw that would break their marriage's back. He asked his parish priest for guidance regarding contraception. The priest told the man that while the Church does teach that contraception is evil, it makes exceptions for cases like his. It was at this point, as he was recounting—reliving—his experience, he broke down, and through tears said, "I wish I had never listened to him. I got snipped. We never had any more children. I regret it." As he finished, another man, also while shedding tears of regret, shared a similar story, in which another priest also said that the Church allowed men in his stressful situation to use contraception for the purpose of saving their marriage. In other words, it is okay to use an illicit means for a good end—which in not correct (see chapter 1).

One of the reasons I facilitated men's retreats centered on St. John Paul II's Theology of the Body was because I also had a similar experience.

After my wife, Kim, and I were married, she had given birth to our first three children within three and a half years; the last of which was extracted out of her womb by means of an emergency C-section. The surgery became complicated, demanding that the surgeon cut through Kim's abdomen both horizontally and vertically, literally opening up her entire belly. Afterward, my wife's obstetrician warned us that she should not become pregnant for at least a year, maybe a year and a half, for fear that she could hemorrhage and perhaps endanger her life.

From that point on, I was looked upon by my wife as a threat. For the most part, we ceased to have sexual relations. Our marriage underwent severe emotional duress. One year became two years; two years became three years of abstinence.

I pleaded with Kim that we seek advice from a priest or a counselor to help us overcome her fears, but she was not interested.

Reaching a tipping point, I decided that I could not endure the situation any longer. It was time for me to move on. Kim took our three daughters to the grocery store. After they left, I packed my bag, and as I was exiting the front door, Kim pulled up. Evidently, as divine providence would have it, she forgot something.

Looking at the bag in my hand, she asked me where I was going. I explained to her that I could not take it anymore and it was time for me to leave. She pleaded with me to stay and promised that she would be willing to talk to a priest about our situation.

We acted fast. That night a local parish priest paid us a visit. The three of us sat at the dining-room table. Kim and I took turns explaining our situation. After we had finished, the priest took a deep breath and responded, "This is easy. The two of you have been faithful to God. You have given Him three beautiful daughters. What more could He ask of you? He does not want the two of you to feel this way. *Humanae Vitae* makes a provision for couples like yourself, who, enduring emotional hardship, are allowed to use contraception. Be at peace."

Kim and I looked at each other. For the first time in a long time, perhaps years, we actually agreed on something . . . we agreed to disagree with this pastoral priest.

Later that week, I attended daily Mass. As I walked toward the church, a man I didn't know, who was standing by his car, called to me, "Hey, you! Come here. I've got something for you." I thought that I had seen him at Mass before, so I went over to him. He handed me an album containing audio tapes (can you tell how old I am?) about John Paul II's Theology of the Body.

I put in that first tape and I was hooked. I began to understand the true meaning of being a man. I discovered that I was to defeat lust in my heart, bear my wife's burdens as my own, be an image of Christ the Bridegroom who lays down His life for His bride, the Church. I realized that responsibility is always connected to suffering and sacrifice; and it is this sacrificial love that unites the husband and wife.

We were obedient. We responded to God's command not to use contraception, and miraculously, God provided the remedy that we needed. After twenty-five years of marriage, I can say with complete honesty that I am more in love with Kim than ever before, and the joy that we have is beyond what I could have hoped for. Not to mention that we have two more beautiful daughters who mean the world to me. I cannot imagine my life without any of them.

Oftentimes, we know what the Church teaches, which is what God commands. But we think we cannot handle the command, and so we seek a minister of God who is a softy, who is pastoral and bends the rules. We get his approval to "do it just this once" and believe that just because a "man of God" said it was okay, God has blessed the decision.

The question is, when people who represent God and His authority teach things contrary to God and his law, must we obey them?

The simple answer is no. "We ought to obey God, rather than men" (Acts 5:29). This Scripture verse is highly appropriate for this discussion because these words are St. Peter's response to the high priest and the Sanhedrin, who forbid him to preach about Jesus Christ. Peter disobeys the religious authorities because they are being disobedient to God.

St. Thomas tells us that there are two circumstances when disobedience to a superior is actually obedience to God: "Sometimes the things commanded by a superior are against God and therefore superiors are not to be obeyed in all things." This includes religious authorities such as popes, cardinals, bishops, and priests.

St. Thomas cites St. Augustine, who argues, "If a commissioner issues an order, are you to comply, if it is contrary to the bidding of the proconsul? Again, if the proconsul commands one thing, and the emperor another, will you hesitate, to disregard the former and serve the latter? Therefore if the emperor commands one thing and God another, you must disregard the former and obey God."[40]

The second circumstance is on matters of the internal soul. For example, a person may be obedient to his superior in external acts, but in decisions within the soul, the superior has no power over his subject. The example Thomas uses is a child who, while living under his parent's authority, must obey them. However, the parents cannot dictate whether their son become a priest or get married.[41] Again, in matters of the internal will, the subject obeys God alone.

This counsel could not be more appropriate for our current global situation. As I write this, the Covid restrictions press on in full force from the highest levels of government. After a year of restrictions, some nations and some of the United States and their governing bodies continue to ban Catholics from gathering to worship and pray.

The question arises: "Are we as Catholics obligated to obey the secular authorities' decision? No. We obey God rather than men.[42]

Yet, the situation becomes difficult to navigate when a bishop, who is God's representative, complies with the government, and propagates the mandate that his flock cannot convene for worship. What is a Catholic to do?

St. Paul says that "If you be risen with Christ seek the things that are above; where Christ is sitting at the right hand of God: Mind the things that are above, not the things that are upon earth. For you are dead and your life is hidden with Christ in God" (Col 3:2–3).

Unfortunately, many a churchman is focused on the things that are below rather than the things that are above. They have forgotten to be concerned with their own resurrection (to be risen with Christ) or the resurrection of others. How can we justify the decision to close down churches and ban the Holy Sacrifice of the Mass, and deny people the sacramental means for their salvation (the things that are above)?

St. Paul is clear: seek the things that are above—*not* the things below. We are to look forward to heaven, to eternal communion with God, even and especially by embracing death. But we hold on to the earth—tightly. We are afraid of the cross. We think it is too demanding.

St. Jose Maria Escriva said, "For us to reach God, Christ is the way; but Christ is on the Cross, and to climb up to the Cross we must have our heart free, not tied to earthly things."[43] Even things as wonderful as our health and earthly existence. The "risen man" that St. Paul references does not suffer the governmental restrictions to hinder him from worshipping the Lord his God.

Plastered on the windows of our church doors are signs that say, "They will know we are Christians by our love." Accordingly, staying home and refraining from gathering to worship is to love. It sounds nice, but no one is inspired by pusillanimity, fear, or the love of the world. No. They will know we are Christians by our courageous charitable obedience to God.

If you are a bishop, seek the things that are above. Courageously inspire and exhort your flock to do the same. .

The Church is to resist fear and those who impose fear upon us. Recall that the members of the early Church often risked their lives to attend the *Eucharistia*. Undaunted, unwavering, and obedient unto God, they sought the things that are above—even to the bitter end of martyrdom. Those who risk not gain not. Comfort makes cowards of us all.

Shepherds of the Church must maintain separation between the Church and the state. They are to be like Tolkien's wizard, Gandalf, who stands on the bridge of *khazad dum*, in the breech between the members of the fellowship and the

Balrog of Moriah, the demon of fire.

Gandalf slams the end of the staff into the rock of the bridge, and defiantly yells to the Balrog, "You shall not pass!" Gandalf is willing to sacrifice his life that his own can go free.

No Catholic bishop is obliged to comply with a government mandate to bar the gates of his churches and shut them down. Why? Because the government is not God, but rather subject to God and His Church. Our bishops are to stand in obedience to God by being disobedient to men, in the spirit of Gandalf, digging in their heals, stating, "You shall not pass!"

St. Joseph is Terror of Demons because nothing—not Herod, not devils, nor the potential scandal of Mary's pregnancy—would deter him from obeying God and protecting the virgin from the consequences of being pregnant prior to the second stage of Jewish marriage, which was stoning; and because of his obedience, Joseph literally became the savior of the Savior.

What about you? What about me? Will we become like St. Joseph? To do so, we must first learn to listen to God by entering the silence daily. If we enter the silence daily, eventually God will grant us the ability to discern his divine guidance.

Second, it is imperative that we know what the Church teaches. Don't take any wooden nickels from wolves in sheep's clothing. Do your research. And whatever you do, don't look for a priest who will give you an escape clause from following the commands of God. By doing so, you may avoid short-term pain, but will inevitably endure long-term suffering.

Third, subject yourself to the duties and responsibilities demanded by your vocation. Don't look outside your vocation for the "big mission." There are enough sacrifices at home as a father, a mother, or a discerning youth. Be faithful to the small matters of your vocation and God will grant you greater responsibilities.

As Fr. Jean-Pierre de Caussade taught,[44] we are to be obedient to God by simply obeying His will in the present moment. Don't fret about the future—it only brings anxiety. Don't live in the past—it only brings depression. Live in the present, for it is a gift from God, through which He speaks directly to you. By living in the present moment of God's will, you can see clearly what God is asking of you and have a keener ability to respond with prompt obedience. Fourth, when you are called to act in obedience, be like St. Joseph and do it with promptness. Promptness is the key characteristic of the obedient man.

Remember that the world's chaos can be remedied by one simple thing: prompt obedience. If we really desire peace and order to reign in our world, then obedience must begin with us. Obedience's power is found in prompt obedience to God and His will, and where there is prompt obedience there exists God's power.

CHAPTER 6

Receiving Power

W ell, you made it. You have nearly completed this little book. It would seem fair to say that we have outlined a road map for achieving and obtaining power. We simply need to be obedient like St. Joseph, channel our passions like St. Joseph, be secret like St. Joseph, be just like St. Joseph, and then we will be powerful.

While it is true that all of these things are absolutely necessary attributes of a person of power, it would not be entirely correct to say that by doing these things we acquire power.

Power, at least God's power, is different than worldly power. God's power is not something you achieve as much as something you receive. Power is not something you can earn as much as something you are given.

Power is a gift from God. But there is an important qualification regarding this gift: God doesn't hand out power like people hand out Halloween candy. God doesn't hand out His power to everyone who rings His doorbell looking for a handout.

God shares His power of virtue only with the humble, because the humble are the only people who are spiritually strong enough, wise enough, and thankful enough to wield the power of virtue.

A large part of humility is being receptive to God and all that He wills. The humble person doesn't reject God's gifts, regardless of whether they arrive packaged in suffering, trials, and tests, or in the Magi's treasures of gold, frankincense, myrrh, and government stimulus checks.

The humble man is absolutely resolutely determined not only to accept all things from God, but also to "be thankful in all circumstances." In fact, St. Paul says, "This is God's will for you, to be thankful in all circumstances" (1 Thes 5:18). It is God's will that we be thankful for His will in all circumstances.

The humble person can see in present pain, future perfection; in current trials, future triumphs; in dying to oneself, a resurrected glory.

Now this type of thinking may appear backward, illogical. The world is chock-full of examples of people who fight for every square inch of their territory; who scrap for every dime and dollar; who dominate, manipulate, coerce, and flatter to obtain what they desire—and sometimes they acquire it. The world's maxim is "survival of the fittest"; "second place is first loser"; "last one in is the rotten egg."

There is an odd irony to the world's understanding and formulation of power. This formulation is most accurately expressed by Machiavelli, who taught that one is to use every and any means available to acquire power. Machiavelli was audacious enough to contend that one should use and abuse the goodness of religion and even God Himself to achieve power.

The irony of Machiavelli's proposal is that it betrays those who abide by his philosophy. When people use goodness and God to acquire power, they may acquire some kind of power, but lose goodness and God in the process. When people grasp for, cling to, and claw and scratch for power, they become an addictive slave to that desire for power. In effect, they become powerless over their desire for power.

Power rules them, and rules out every type of goodness that is derived from self-giving love. Our Lord speaks about such miserable individuals: "Unless a grain of wheat falling to the ground die, itself remains alone" (Jn 12:24). Like a king on his throne with his scepter in hand, he has all of the power, with no one but himself to rule. People simply hate being around people who don't know how to serve. The only reason people remain with those who crave worldly power is because they believe they can sponge some of that power for themselves.

The irony is that the power betrays our powerful king. Rather than him ruling with power, his power rules him. In the end he is alone . . . with his power having power over him.

The person who is receptive to God, on the other hand, who finds and accepts God's will in all things and circumstances presented to him, is the one who is truly powerful. He is not bound or enslaved by a perennial desire for power, but rather uses all in his power to achieve union with God. Power is a means to goodness and to God, rather than vice versa.

Such a man is not enslaved to power but free to receive all things from God, which gives him power over being attached to his selfishness and persistent self-will.

At this point someone might object, "Simply receiving from God is great, as long as He gives me things that are good, and the things that I desire. But what if He stops giving? Or gives to me that which I don't want?"

The very question presupposes a lack of trust in God. Why do we mistrust God when He loves us more than we love ourselves? Why do we not trust the all-knowing God whose plan is better than our limited vision for our lives?

The point is this: either you believe that God is love and that He loves you infinitely and desires the best for you, or you don't. If you don't believe that God wants the best for you, your only option is to believe that rather than being a collaborator, He is your competitor; and that He exists to make your life miserable.

If you take the latter route and view God as your competitor, you will eventually jockey and grasp to obtain some kind of worldly power, rather than trustingly being receptive to God and the power He wills to give you.

St. Joseph was a master at being receptive before God. He accepted God's will in circumstances that, by all human assessment, were devastating, only to come out gloriously perfected.

St. Matthew's Gospel tells us that "Joseph arising from sleep did what the angel of the Lord commanded and took Mary his wife" (Mt 1:24).

Initially, it sounds like Joseph took control of the situation by "taking" Mary. The Greek word that is translated as "took," *paralabon*, actually means *to receive*. Joseph didn't take anything. He received Mary as a gift from God. St. Joseph did not grasp for or attempt to control Mary. When he discovered Mary pregnant without his cooperation, rather than clinging to Mary and attempting to maintain control of her, he surrendered the awkward and alarming situation to God and waited for God to direct him.

This is important because St. Joseph teaches us by his example something essential regarding power: power is associated not with conquest and taking, but with receptivity before God. And yet, there is another lesson: St. Joseph's example teaches us that we receive power the way he did—through Mary.

If St. Joseph had decided not to receive Mary, he would not have become the virginal father of the Son of God. He would not have received she who is preeminent in grace. Without Mary, St. Joseph would not have received his call to fatherly greatness; he would not have received Christ himself; he would not have become head of the Holy Family or patron of the Universal Church.

By receiving Mary, Joseph received a vast number of graces—too many to attempt to recount in this little chapter.

Before I proceed, it is important to mention that popes, theologians, mystics, scholars, and devotees have written extensively and prolifically on the subject of the Blessed Virgin Mary. Considering this, there is no legitimate reason for me to expound on the glories of Mary here. The purpose of this chapter is to demonstrate succinctly that to Joseph, Mary became a "distributor of God's manifold grace" (see 1 Pet 4:10) and power; and that by doing as he did, we too can receive this power from her.

Consider that Mary is the beloved and chosen daughter of God the Father. Mary was overshadowed by (at the Annunciation) and received the plenitude of grace from (during her conception) the Holy Spirit. Mary conceived by the Holy Spirit and became the Holy Virgin Mother of God the Son.

Each Person of the Trinity has a uniquely intimate relationship with Mary. The Trinity converges on Mary. Mary is God's holy dwelling place.

This is confirmed by the angel Gabriel's salutation to her, "Hail full of grace, the Lord is with thee!" (Lk 1:26). God the Father, God the Son, God the Holy Spirit, the One God is always in, and perpetually with, Mary.

In the Israelites' wanderings in the desert, Moses erected the Tent of Meeting. Within the Tent of Meeting, behind the curtain, located in the holy of holies, was the Ark.

God commanded Moses to make the Ark of the Lord from acacia wood and covered it in gold. The ark was approximately two yards wide by three yards long and was cherished as containing the very presence of God, for it contained the Ten Commandments; the manna from heaven in an urn; and Aaron's staff that budded an almond shoot. The glory cloud, the Holy Spirit, overshadowed (Greek, *episkiasei*) the Ark of the Lord.

The Ark was Israel's secret weapon; it was often carried into battle, winning for the Jews decisive and often impossible victories. It was the Ark of the Lord that caused the walls of Jericho to crumble. When the Israelites, led by Joshua, entered the promised land, it was the Ark, carried by the Levitical priests, that caused the waters of the Jordan to congeal at the city of Adam, enabling the Israelites to cross the riverbed dry-shod.

St. Luke, in his Gospel, draws a parallel association between the Ark of the Lord and Mary. The same Holy Spirit that overshadowed the Ark, overshadowed (*episkiasei*) Mary. Mary contained the fulfillment of the ancient Ark's possessions: Jesus, the Word of God (the fulfillment of the Ten Commandments); the Bread of Life (the fulfillment of the manna from heaven); and the priesthood of Jesus (the fulfillment of the Levitical priesthood), the one who would rule the nations with an iron rod, the shoot of David (prefigured by Aaron's staff that budded an almond shoot).

Indeed, as David proclaimed, 'Who am I that the Ark of the Lord should come to me?' When Mary greeted her pregnant cousin Elizabeth, Elizabeth cried out, 'Who am I that the mother of my Lord should come to me?' The word Luke uses for "to cry out" (*anephonesen*) is an uncommon word, only used in Sacred Scripture in the context of a liturgical celebration wherein the Ark of the Lord was present. In other words, Luke is indicating that Mary is the fulfillment of the Ark of the Lord.[45]

This is an elaborate way of saying that like the Tent of Meeting and the Ark that was within the Tent of Meeting, Mary is God's tent—God's meeting place; God's ark—His holy dwelling place. Joseph encountered God in and through Mary.

Mary becomes the "meeting place"; the place where St. Joseph encountered God, in and through her. The Blessed Virgin Mary is the nexus between the Trinity and St. Joseph, between God and all of us.

Not only is Mary the place of encounter between God and man, but she is also a reservoir of overflowing grace. Scripture tells us that the angel Gabriel addressed Mary, not with the name that her parents gave her, but rather by the title *kecharitomene*, which is a unique Greek word used only once in the entirety of Scripture, and it is addressed only to the Holy Virgin. It is the past perfect tense of making one full of grace; meaning that Mary was made, in her conception, perfect, in an ongoing manner full of grace, without any sin or moral blemish.

Again, Mary is not only the "meeting place" of God and man but is also a reservoir of grace. She literally is full of grace and overflowing with grace for all who are willing to drink from her.

With St. Joseph we are to go to the "meeting place" of Mary if we are to receive the grace of God.

St. Joseph received and receives God and grace though Mary; and we, if we are humble enough to submit to her, also will receive God and God's grace through this Holy Virgin Mother.

St. Joseph received his vocation as a husband, his role as protector and provider, head and servant of the Holy Family. Through Mary, Joseph received his fatherhood and achieved his manhood, and by means of his continual self-donation to her and Jesus, his sainthood.

Through Mary, Joseph received both trial and triumphs; riches from the Magi and persecutions from Herod; the hardship of exile and the joy of a happy homelife.

St. Joseph was the first person to entrust himself, consecrate himself, to Mary. This humble act of receiving Mary into his home inaugurated Joseph's path to glory.

Mary obtained every grace necessary for Joseph's incredible sanctification, holiness, and virtue, by her prayers, mortifications, intercession, and her unique relationship with all three divine Persons of the Trinity.

If we want holiness, sanctity, and the ability to conquer sin and vanquish the devil, we must do what Joseph did: entrust our entire life, our marriages, our families to Mary.

This is my experience. During the early years of my marriage, I struggled to embrace my fatherly vocation. It wasn't that I didn't love my wife or my children. I simply didn't understand how to be a great father or appreciate the greatness of fatherhood.

A friend took me to Medjugorje. Prior to that trip, I completed St. Louis de Montfort's formula of consecration to Jesus through Mary. While I was in Medjugorje I had a conversation with a wonderful woman name Nancy. I confessed that I had a desire to serve the Lord, but I didn't know how to actuate it, make it real.

She asked, "Are you married?" (I don't think she asked this because she was interested in me.)

"Yes, I am married."

"Do you have children?"

"Yes, I have three."

"Go home and be St. Joseph."

I have never forgot that exhortation.

After returning from that trip, I asked Mary to introduce me to St. Joseph, and what transpired since then is inexplicable. Mary introduced me to St. Joseph, and St. Joseph led me more deeply into the mystery of Mary and Jesus. It was as if, through St. Joseph, I could envision the mysteries of the Rosary in high definition, as motion pictures. From that point on, these two parents have led me more deeply into the mysteries of God.

As our parents in the order of grace, Mary and Joseph do for us what they did for Christ, who could not do it for Himself. As they consecrated the child Jesus to God that He may be sacred unto God, so also these parents consecrate us, through Jesus, with Jesus, and in Jesus, to God, that we may be made sacred unto the Lord, and consecrated for a specific purpose in His holy plan.

I could go on at length describing the many graces I have received through these holy parents, but it would demand another book. The main point is that through Mary, in union with St. Joseph, God gives real power to overcome the devil and his minions.

If you desire true virtue, God's power, go to Mary with Joseph, and entrust yourself to the care of these, your parents in Christ. Receive Mary as Joseph did, and with her you will receive the power to conquer yourself, the devil, and vanquish the very powers of hell. You will experience the power of St. Joseph and be like him, a Terror of Demons.

ENDNOTES

1 https://www.oxfordbibliographies.com/view/document/obo-9780195393361/obo-9780195393361-0006.xml, accessed March 19, 2021. "The title 'apocryphal gospels' conventionally applies to certain early Christian or Gnostic texts that are written either in imitation of the genre "gospel" as applied to the New Testament canon or in telling of events and sayings in the life of Jesus and his immediate circle of family and disciples. The pluralism of the centuries of Christianity, the absence of a clearly established canon, the role of orality and intertextuality in the shaping of the new texts, and the existence of different 'editions' of even the future canonical texts also doubtless encouraged the writing of Christian apocrypha. Modern critical editions of the texts are collected into compendia under umbrella titles such as New Testament Apocrypha or the Nag Hammadi Library. Some texts, such as the Gospel of Thomas, have been extensively studied and have spawned a vast secondary literature. Others are only recently undergoing scholarly examination. Some of the texts, for example the Gospel of Judas, have come to light only recently. Others, such as the Protevangelium of James, have survived in numerous manuscript copies, some of great antiquity, and those have been known to scholars for centuries. Some texts are fragmentary; the smallest examples raise the question whether they are indeed chance survivors of a larger gospel-type writing or should really be classed as something else, perhaps part of a patristic writing or homily. The texts selected here are largely orthodox. Only a few are Gnostic: the Gospel of Philip, the Gospel of Judas, and the Gospel of Mary; the famous Gospel of Thomas has been considered Gnostic by many readers. Most of the remaining Gnostic gospels have been included in a final section on their own."

2 https://www.newadvent.org/cathen/15472a.htm, accessed March 19, 2021.

3 St. Thomas Aquinas, Summa Theologica, Secunda Secundae, q 58.

4 Ibid.

5 Ibid.

6 St. Thomas Aquinas, Summa Theologica, Secunda Secundae, q 58.
   "Consequently there must be one supreme virtue essentially distinct
   from every other virtue, which directs all the virtues to the common
   good; and this virtue is legal justice."

7 St. Thomas Aquinas, Summa Theologica, Secunda Secundae, q 58.

8 https://plato.stanford.edu/entries/justice-virtue, accessed March 19, 2021.

9 St. Thomas Aquinas, Summa Theologica, Secunda Secundae, q 58.

10 Ibid.

11 Ibid.

12 Jude P. Dougherty; "Keeping the Common Good in Mind," The ethics
   of St. Thomas Aquinas, p. 197.

13 Ibid.

14 Ibid.

15 Ibid.

16 Ibid.

17 See Lev 20:10; Num 5:16-27

18 Ibid.

19 https://onepeterfive.com/negativity-is-a-drug-and-were-hooked,
   accessed March 19, 2021.

20 St. Thomas Aquinas, Summa Theologica, Secunda Secundae, q 132.

21 Ibid.

22 Ibid.

23 Ibid.

24 Ibid.

25 Ibid.

26 Ibid.

27 Ibid.

28 https://www.artofmanliness.com/articles/got-thumos, accessed March 19, 2021.

29 Ibid.

30 Ibid.

31 St. Thomas Aquinas,Summa Theologica, Secunda Secundae, q 23.

32 Ibid.

33 https://www.artofmanliness.com/articles/got-thumos, accessed March 19, 2021.

34 Enthymeomai, Bible Hub, online edition, www.biblehub.com/greek/1760.htm, accessed March 19, 2021.

35 St. Thomas Aquinas, Summa Theologica, Secunda Secundae, q 23.

36 St. Thomas Aquinas, Summa Theologica, Secunda Secundae, q 23.

37 Sacred Congregation of Rites, Decr. Quemadmodum Deus (December 8, 1970): p.282.

38 Devin Schadt, The Meaning and Mystery of Man, 131.

39 St. Thomas Aquinas, Summa Theologica, Secunda Secundae, q 23.

40 Ibid.

41 Ibid.

42 Ibid.

43 Josemaria Escriva, The Way of the Cross, Scepter, 88.

44 Paul Garvin, Trustful Surrender to Divine Providence: The Secret of Peace and Happiness, TAN.

45 Devin Schadt, Custos: Total Consecration Through Saint Joseph, 56-57.

KNOW YOUR **PURPOSE.**
BUILD YOUR **PLAN.**
UNLOCK THE **POWER.**

The Fathers of St. Joseph has developed a plan that helps men know their noble purpose and unlock God's power in their lives. Access the tools to help you become who God intended you to be—like St. Joseph, a father on earth like the Father in Heaven at:

FATHERSOFSTJOSEPH.ORG